Cascading Style Sheets Specification, Level 1

W3C Recommendation 17 Dec 1996, revised 11 Jan 1999

REC-CSS1-19990111

This book made available through
a workshop sponsored by
**South Central
Regional Library Council**

Cascading Style Sheets Specification, Level 1

W3C Recommendation 17 Dec 1996, revised 11 Jan 1999

REC-CSS1-19990111

Open Docs Library

San Jose   New York   Lincoln   Shanghai

Cascading Style Sheets Specification, Level 1

REC-CSS1-19990111
W3C Recommendation 17 Dec 1996,

Compiled from the W3C Standards by Gordon McComb

Published by Open Docs Library, an imprint of iUniverse.com, Inc.

Massachusetts Institute of Technology, Institut National de Recherché en
Informatique et en Automatique, Keio University
http://www.w3.org/Consortium/Legal/

For information address:
iUniverse.com, Inc.

620 North 48th Street

Suite 201

Lincoln, NE 68504-3467

www.iuniverse.com

ISBN: 1-58348-252-0
LCCN: 99-63371

Printed in the United States of America

Contents

This version:

   `http://www.w3.org/TR/1999/REC-CSS1-19990111`

Latest version:

   `http://www.w3.org/TR/REC-CSS1`

Previous version:

   `http://www.w3.org/TR/REC-CSS1-961217`

Authors:

   `Håkon Wium Lie (howcome@w3.org)`
   `Bert Bos (bert@w3.org)`

Status of this document

This document is a W3C Recommendation. It has been reviewed by W3C (http://www.w3.org/) Members and general consensus that the specification is appropriate for use has been reached. It is a stable document and may be used as reference material or cited as a normative reference from another document. W3C promotes widespread deployment of this Recommendation.

A list of current W3C Recommendations and other technical documents can be found at http://www.w3.org/TR/.

This document is a revised version of the document first released on 17 December 1996. Changes from the original version are listed in Appendix F. *The list of known errors in this specification is available at* http://www.w3.org/Style/CSS/Errata/REC-CSS1-19990111-errata

Abstract

This document specifies level 1 of the Cascading Style Sheet mechanism (CSS1). CSS1 is a simple style sheet mechanism that allows authors and readers to attach style (e.g. fonts, colors and spacing) to HTML documents. The CSS1 language is human readable and writable, and expresses style in common desktop publishing terminology.

One of the fundamental features of CSS is that style sheets cascade; authors can attach a preferred style sheet, while the reader may have a personal style sheet to adjust for human or technological handicaps. The rules for resolving conflicts between different style sheets are defined in this specification.

This Recommendation results from W3C activities in the area of Style Sheets. For background information on style sheets, see [1].

Terminology

attribute

    HTML attribute

author

    the author of an HTML document

block-level element

    an element which has a line break before and after (e.g. 'H1' in HTML)

canvas

    the part of the UA's drawing surface onto which documents are rendered

child element

    a *subelement* in SGML [5] terminology

contextual selector

    a selector that matches elements based on their position in the document structure. A contextual selector consists of several simple selectors. E.g., the contextual selector 'H1.initial B' consists of two simple selectors, 'H1.initial' and 'B'.

CSS

    Cascading Style Sheets

CSS1

    Cascading Style Sheets, level 1. This document defines CSS1 which is a simple style sheet mechanism for the web.

CSS1 advanced features

    features that are described in this specification but labeled as not among the CSS1 core features

CSS1 core features

the part of CSS1 that is required in all CSS1 conforming UAs

CSS1 parser

a User Agent that reads CSS1 style sheets

declaration

a property (e.g. 'font-size') and a corresponding value (e.g. '12pt')

designer

the designer of a style sheet

document

HTML document

element

HTML element

element type

a *generic identifier* in SGML [5] terminology

fictional tag sequence

a tool for describing the behavior of pseudo-classes and pseudo-elements

font size

The size for which a font is designed. Typically, the size of a font is approximately equal to the distance from the bottom of the lowest letter with a descender to the top of the tallest letter with an ascender and (optionally) with a diacritical mark.

HTML

Hypertext Markup Language [2], an application of SGML.

HTML extension

Markup introduced by UA vendors, most often to support certain visual effects. The "FONT", "CENTER" and "BLINK" elements are examples of HTML extensions, as is the "BGCOLOR" attribute. One of the goals of CSS is to provide an alternative to HTML extensions.

inline element

an element which does not have a line break before and after (e.g. 'STRONG' in HTML)

intrinsic dimensions

the width and height as defined by the element itself, not imposed by the surroundings. In this specification it is assumed that all replaced elements— and only replaced elements— come with intrinsic dimensions.

parent element

the *containing element* in SGML [5] terminology

pseudo-element

pseudo-elements are used in CSS selectors to address typographical items (e.g. the first line of an element) rather than structural elements.

pseudo-class

pseudo-classes are used in CSS selectors to allow information external to the HTML source (e.g. the fact that an anchor has been visited or not) to classify elements.

property

a stylistic parameter that can be influenced through CSS. This specification defines a list of properties and their corresponding values.

reader

the person for whom the document is rendered

replaced element

an element that the CSS formatter only knows the intrinsic dimensions of. In HTML, 'IMG', 'INPUT', 'TEXTAREA', 'SELECT' and 'OBJECT' elements can be examples of replaced elements. E.g., the content of the 'IMG' element is often replaced by the image that the SRC attribute points to. CSS1 does not define how the intrinsic dimensions are found.

rule

a declaration (e.g. 'font-family: helvetica') and its selector (e.g. 'H1')

selector

a string that identifies what elements the corresponding rule applies to. A selector can either be a simple selector (e.g. 'H1') or a contextual selector (e.g. 'H1 B') which consists of several simple selectors.

SGML

Standard Generalized Markup Language [5], of which HTML is an application

simple selector

a selector that matches elements based on the element type and/or attributes, and not he element's position in the document structure. E.g., 'H1.initial' is a simple selector.

style sheet

a collection of rules

UA

User Agent, often a *web browser* or *web client*

user

synonymous with *reader*

weight

the priority of a rule

In the text of this specification, single quotes ('...') denote HTML and CSS excerpts.

Copyright Notice

Introduction

What are style sheets?

Style sheets describe how documents are presented on screens, in print, or perhaps how they are pronounced. W3C has actively promoted the use of style sheets on the Web since the Consortium was founded in 1994. The Style Sheets Activity has produced two W3C Recommendations (CSS1 and CSS2) which are widely, although not consistently, implemented in browsers.

By attaching style sheets to structured documents on the Web (e.g. HTML), authors and readers can influence the presentation of documents without sacrificing device-independence or adding new HTML tags.

The easiest way to start experimenting with style sheets is to find a browser that support CSS. Discussions about style sheets are carried out on the www-style@w3.org mailing list and on comp.infosystems.www.authoring.stylesheets.

The W3C Style Sheets Activity is also developing XSL.

Why Two Style Sheet languages?

The fact that W3C has started developing XSL in addition to CSS has caused some confusion. Why develop a second style sheet language when implementors haven't even finished the first one? The answer can be found in the table below:

Function	CSS	XSL
Can be used with HTML?	yes	no
Can be used with XML?	yes	yes
Transformation language?	no	yes
Syntax	CSS	XML

The unique features are that CSS can be used to style HTML documents. XSL, on the other hand, is able to tranform documents. For example, XSL can be used to transform XML data into HTML/CSS documents on the Web server. This way, the two languages complement each other and can be used together.

Both languages can be used to style XML documents.

CSS and XSL will use the same underlying formatting model and designers will therefore have access to the same formatting features in both languages. W3C will work hard to ensure that interoperable implementations of the formatting model is available.

A W3C Note on "Using XSL and CSS together" is available.

XSL

W3C has launched a Working Group to develop the eXtensible Style Language (XSL). XSL builds on DSSSL and CSS and is primarily targeted for highly structured XML data which e.g. needs element reordering before presentation. For more information on XSL see the W3C XSL resource page.

Dynamic HTML

Dynamic HTML is a term used to describe HTML pages with dynamic content. CSS is one of three components in dynamic HTML; the other two are HTML itself and JavaScript (which is being standardized under the name EcmaScript). The three components are glued together with DOM, the Document Object Model. Dynamic HTML is still in its infancy and current implementations are experimental.

Chapter 1

Basic Concepts

Designing simple style sheets is easy. One needs only to know a little HTML and some basic desktop publishing terminology. E.g., to set the text color of 'H1' elements to blue, one can say:

```
H1 { color: blue }
```

The example above is a simple CSS rule. A rule consists of two main parts: selector ('H1') and declaration ('color: blue'). The declaration has two parts: property ('color') and value ('blue'). While the example above tries to influence only one of the properties needed for rendering an HTML document, it qualifies as a style sheet on its own. Combined with other style sheets (one fundamental feature of CSS is that style sheets are combined) it will determine the final presentation of the document.

The selector is the link between the HTML document and the style sheet, and all HTML element types are possible selectors. HTML element types are defined in the HTML specification [2].

The 'color' property is one of around 50 properties that determine the presentation of an HTML document. The list of properties and their possible values is defined in this specification.

HTML authors need to write style sheets only if they want to suggest a specific style for their documents. Each User Agent (UA, often a "web browser" or "web client") will have a default style sheet that presents documents in a reasonable — but arguably mundane — manner. Appendix A contains a sample style sheet to present HTML documents as suggested in the HTML 2.0 specification [3].

The formal grammar for the CSS1 language is defined in Appendix B.

1.1 Containment in HTML

In order for the style sheets to influence the presentation, the UA must be aware of their existence. The HTML specification [2] define how to link HTML with style sheets. This section is therefore informative, but not normative:

```
<HTML>
  <HEAD>
    <TITLE>title</TITLE>
    <LINK REL=STYLESHEET TYPE="text/css"
```

```
      HREF="http://style.com/cool" TITLE="Cool">
    <STYLE TYPE="text/css">
      @import url(http://style.com/basic);
      H1 { color: blue }
    </STYLE>
  </HEAD>
  <BODY>
    <H1>Headline is blue</H1>
    <P STYLE="color: green">While the paragraph is green.
  </BODY>
</HTML>
```

The example shows four ways to combine style and HTML: using the 'LINK' element to link an external style sheet, a 'STYLE' element inside the 'HEAD' element, an imported style sheet using the CSS '@import' notation, and a 'STYLE' attribute on an element inside 'BODY'. The latter option mixes style with content and loses the corresponding advantages of traditional style sheets.

The 'LINK' element references alternative style sheets that the reader can select, while imported style sheets are automatically merged with the rest of the style sheet.

Traditionally, UAs have silently ignored unknown tags. As a result, old UAs will ignore the 'STYLE' element, but its content will be treated as part of the document body, and rendered as such. During a transition phase, 'STYLE' element content may be hidden using SGML comments:

```
<STYLE TYPE="text/css"><!-
  H1 { color: green }
-></STYLE>
```

Since the 'STYLE' element is declared as "CDATA" in the DTD (as defined in [2]), conforming SGML parsers will not consider the above style sheet to be a comment that is to be removed.

1.2 Grouping

To reduce the size of style sheets, one can group selectors in comma-separated lists:

```
H1, H2, H3 { font-family: helvetica }
```

Similarly, declarations can be grouped:

```
H1 {
  font-weight: bold;
```

```
    font-size: 12pt;
    line-height: 14pt;
    font-family: helvetica;
    font-variant: normal;
    font-style: normal;
}
```

In addition, some properties have their own grouping syntax:

```
H1 { font: bold 12pt/14pt helvetica }
```

which is equivalent to the previous example.

1.3 Inheritance

In the first example, the color of 'H1' elements was set to blue. Suppose there is an 'H1' element with an emphasized element inside:

```
<H1>The headline <EM>is</EM> important!</H1>
```

If no color has been assigned to the 'EM' element, the emphasized "is" will inherit the color of the parent element, i.e. it will also appear in blue. Other style properties are likewise inherited, e.g. 'font-family' and 'font-size'.

To set a "default" style property for a document, one can set the property on an element from which all visible elements descend. In HTML documents, the 'BODY' element can serve this function:

```
BODY {
    color: black;
    background: url(texture.gif) white;
}
```

This will work even if the author has omitted the 'BODY' tag (which is legal) since the HTML parser will infer the missing tag. The example above sets the text color to be black and the background to be an image. The background will be white if the image is not available. (See section 5.3 for more on this.)

Some style properties are not inherited from the parent element to the child element. Most often it is intuitive why this is not the case. E.g., the 'background' property does not inherit, but the parent element's background will shine through by default.

Often, the value of a property is a percentage that refers to another property:

```
P { font-size: 10pt }
P { line-height: 120% }   /* relative to 'font-size', i.e. 12pt */
```

For each property that allows percentage values, it is defined what property it refers to. Children elements of 'P' will inherit the computed value of 'line-height' (i.e. 12pt), not the percentage.

1.4 Class as selector

To increase the granularity of control over elements, a new attribute has been added to HTML [2]: 'CLASS'. All elements inside the 'BODY' element can be classed, and the class can be addressed in the style sheet:

```
<HTML>
 <HEAD>
  <TITLE>Title</TITLE>
  <STYLE TYPE="text/css">
    H1.pastoral { color: #00FF00 }
  </STYLE>
 </HEAD>
 <BODY>
  <H1 CLASS=pastoral>Way too green</H1>
 </BODY>
</HTML>
```

The normal inheritance rules apply to classed elements; they inherit values from their parent in the document structure.

One can address all elements of the same class by omitting the tag name in the selector:

```
.pastoral { color: green }   /* all elements with CLASS pastoral */
```

Only one class can be specified per selector. 'P.pastoral.marine' is therefore an invalid selector in CSS1. (Contextual selectors, described below, can have one class per simple selector)

CSS gives so much power to the CLASS attribute, that in many cases it doesn't even matter what HTML element the class is set on — you can make any element emulate almost any other. Relying on this power is not recommended, since it removes the level of structure that has a universal meaning (HTML elements). A structure based on CLASS is only useful within a restricted domain, where the meaning of a class has been mutually agreed upon.

1.5 ID as selector

HTML [2] also introduces the 'ID' attribute which is guaranteed to have a unique value over the document. It can therefore be of special importance as a style sheet selector, and can be addressed with a preceding '#':

```
#z98y { letter-spacing: 0.3em }
H1#z98y { letter-spacing: 0.5em }

<P ID=z98y>Wide text</P>
```

In the above example, the first selector matches the 'P' element due to the 'ID' attribute value. The second selector specifies both an element type ('H1') and an ID value, and will therefore not match the 'P' element.

By using the ID attribute as selector, one can set style properties on a per-element basis. While style sheets have been designed to augment document structure, this feature will allow authors to create documents that present well on the canvas without taking advantage of the structural elements of HTML. This use of style sheets is discouraged.

1.6 Contextual selectors

Inheritance saves CSS designers typing. Instead of setting all style properties, one can create defaults and then list the exceptions. To give 'EM' elements within 'H1' a different color, one may specify:

```
H1 { color: blue }
EM { color: red }
```

When this style sheet is in effect, all emphasized sections within or outside 'H1' will turn red. Probably, one wanted only 'EM' elements within 'H1' to turn red and this can be specified with:

```
H1 EM { color: red }
```

The selector is now a search pattern on the stack of open elements, and this type of selector is referred to as a contextual selector. Contextual selectors consist of several simple selectors separated by whitespace (all selectors described up to now have been simple selectors). Only elements that match the last simple selector (in this case the 'EM' element) are addressed, and only if the search pattern matches. Contextual selectors in CSS1 look for ancestor relationships, but other relationships (e.g. parent-child) may be introduced in later revisions. In the example above, the search pattern matches if 'EM' is a descendant of 'H1', i.e. if 'EM' is inside an 'H1' element.

```
UL LI    { font-size: small }
UL UL LI { font-size: x-small }
```

Here, the first selector matches 'LI' elements with at least one 'UL' ancestor. The second selector matches a subset of the first, i.e. 'LI' elements with at least two 'UL' ancestors. The conflict is resolved by the second selector being more specific because of the longer search pattern. See the cascading order (section 3.2) for more on this.

Contextual selectors can look for element types, CLASS attributes, ID attributes or combinations of these:

```
DIV P            { font: small sans-serif }
.reddish H1      { color: red }
#x78y CODE       { background: blue }
DIV.sidenote H1 { font-size: large }
```

The first selector matches all 'P' elements that have a 'DIV' among the ancestors. The second selector matches all 'H1' elements that have an ancestor of class 'reddish'. The third selector matches all 'CODE' elements that are descendants of the element with 'ID=x78y'. The fourth selector matches all 'H1' elements that have a 'DIV' ancestor with class 'sidenote'.

Several contextual selectors can be grouped together:

```
H1 B, H2 B, H1 EM, H2 EM { color: red }
```

Which is equivalent to:

```
H1 B { color: red }
H2 B { color: red }
H1 EM { color: red }
H2 EM { color: red }
```

1.7 Comments

Textual comments in CSS style sheets are similar to those in the C programming language [7]:

```
EM { color: red }   /* red, really red!! */
```

Comments cannot be nested. For a CSS1 parser, a comment is equivalent to whitespace.

Chapter 2

Pseudo-classes and Pseudo-elements

In CSS1, style is normally attached to an element based on its position in the document structure. This simple model is sufficient for a wide variety of styles, but doesn't cover some common effects. The concept of pseudo-classes and pseudo-elements extend addressing in CSS1 to allow external information to influence the formatting process.

Pseudo-classes and pseudo-elements can be used in CSS selectors, but do not exist in the HTML source. Rather, they are "inserted" by the UA under certain conditions to be used for addressing in style sheets. They are referred to as "classes" and "elements" since this is a convenient way of describing their behavior. More specifically, their behavior is defined by a *fictional tag sequence*.

Pseudo-elements are used to address sub-parts of elements, while pseudo-classes allow style sheets to differentiate between different element types.

2.1 Anchor pseudo-classes

User agents commonly display newly visited anchors differently from older ones. In CSS1, this is handled through pseudo-classes on the 'A' element:

```
A:link { color: red }       /* unvisited link */
A:visited { color: blue }   /* visited links */
A:active { color: lime }    /* active links */
```

All 'A' elements with an 'HREF' attribute will be put into one and only one of these groups (i.e. target anchors are not affected). UAs may choose to move an element from 'visited' to 'link' after a certain time. An 'active' link is one that is currently being selected (e.g. by a mouse button press) by the reader.

The formatting of an anchor pseudo-class is as if the class had been inserted manually. A UA is not required to reformat a currently displayed document due to anchor pseudo-class transitions. E.g., a style sheet can legally specify that the 'font-size' of an 'active' link should be larger than a 'visited' link, but the UA is not required to dynamically reformat the document when the reader selects the 'visited' link.

Pseudo-class selectors do not match normal classes, and vice versa. The style rule in the example below will therefore not have any influence:

```
A:link { color: red }

<A CLASS=link NAME=target5> ... </A>
```

In CSS1, anchor pseudo-classes have no effect on elements other than 'A'. Therefore, the element type can be omitted from the selector:

```
A:link { color: red }
:link { color: red }
```

The two selectors above will select the same elements in CSS1.

Pseudo-class names are case-insensitive.

Pseudo-classes can be used in contextual selectors:

```
A:link IMG { border: solid blue }
```

Also, pseudo-classes can be combined with normal classes:

```
A.external:visited { color: blue }

<A CLASS=external HREF="http://out.side/">external link</A>
```

If the link in the above example has been visited, it will be rendered in blue. Note that normal class names precede pseudo-classes in the selector.

2.2 Typographical pseudo-elements

Some common typographical effects are associated not with structural elements but rather with typographical items as formatted on the canvas. In CSS1, two such typographical items can be addressed through pseudo-elements: the first line of an element, and the first letter.

CSS1 core: UAs may ignore all rules with ':first-line' or ':first-letter' in the selector, or, alternatively, only support a subset of the properties on these pseudo-elements. (see section 7)

2.3 The 'first-line' pseudo-element

The 'first-line' pseudo-element is used to apply special styles to the first line as formatted on the canvas:

```
<STYLE TYPE="text/css">
  P:first-line { font-variant: small-caps }
</STYLE>

<P>The first line of an article in Newsweek.
```

On a text-based UA, this could be formatted as:

```
THE FIRST LINE OF AN
article in Newsweek.
```

The fictional tag sequence in the above example is:

```
<P>
<P:first-line>
The first line of an
</P:first-line>
article in Newsweek.
</P>
```

The 'first-line' end tag is inserted at the end of the first line as formatted on the canvas.

The 'first-line' pseudo-element can only be attached to a block-level element.

The 'first-line' pseudo-element is similar to an inline element, but with certain restrictions. Only the following properties apply to a 'first-line' element: font properties (5.2), color and background properties (5.3), 'word-spacing' (5.4.1), 'letter-spacing' (5.4.2), 'text-decoration' (5.4.3), 'vertical-align' (5.4.4), 'text-transform' (5.4.5), 'line-height' (5.4.8), 'clear' (5.5.26).

2.4 The 'first-letter' pseudo-element

The 'first-letter' pseudo-element is used for "initial caps" and "drop caps", which are common typographical effects. It is similar to an inline element if its 'float' property is 'none', otherwise it is similar to a floating element. These are the properties that apply to 'first-letter' pseudo-elements: font properties (5.2), color and background properties (5.3), 'text-decoration' (5.4.3), 'vertical-align' (only if 'float' is 'none', 5.4.4), 'text-transform' (5.4.5), 'line-height' (5.4.8), margin properties (5.5.1–5.5.5), padding properties (5.5.6–5.5.10), border properties (5.5.11–5.5.22), 'float' (5.5.25), 'clear' (5.5.26).

This is how you could make a dropcap initial letter span two lines:

```
<HTML>
 <HEAD>
  <TITLE>Title</TITLE>
  <STYLE TYPE="text/css">
   P                 { font-size: 12pt; line-height: 12pt }
   P:first-letter { font-size: 200%; float: left }
   SPAN              { text-transform: uppercase }
  </STYLE>
 </HEAD>
 <BODY>
  <P><SPAN>The first</SPAN> few words of an article in The Economist.</P>
 </BODY>
</HTML>
```

If a text-based UA supports the 'first-letter' pseudo-element (they probably will not), the above could be formatted as:

```
___
| HE FIRST few
| words of an
article in the
Economist.
```

The fictional tag sequence is:

```
<P>
<SPAN>
<P:first-letter>
T
</P:first-letter>he first
</SPAN>
few words of an article in the Economist.
</P>
```

Note that the 'first-letter' pseudo-element tags abut the content (i.e. the initial character), while the 'first-line' pseudo-element start tag is inserted right after the start tag of the element it is attached to.

The UA defines what characters are inside the 'first-letter' element. Normally, quotes that precede the first letter should be included:

```
||   /\     bird in
    /  \    the hand
   /----\   is worth
  /      \  two in
the bush," says an
old proverb.
```

When the paragraph starts with other punctuation (e.g. parenthesis and ellipsis points) or other characters that are normally not considered letters (e.g. digits and mathematical symbols), 'first-letter' pseudo-elements are usually ignored.

Some languages may have specific rules about how to treat certain letter combinations. In Dutch, for example, if the letter combination "ij" appears at the beginning of a word, they should both be considered within the 'first-letter' pseudo-element.

The 'first-letter' pseudo-element can only be attached to a block-level element.

2.5 Pseudo-elements in selectors

In a contextual selector, pseudo-elements are only allowed at the end of the selector:

```
BODY P:first-letter { color: purple }
```

Pseudo-elements can be combined with classes in selectors:

```
P.initial:first-letter { color: red }

<P CLASS=initial>First paragraph</A>
```

The above example would make the first letter of all 'P' elements with 'CLASS=initial' red. When combined with classes or pseudo-classes, pseudo-elements must be specified at the end of the selector. Only one pseudo-element can be specified per selector.

2.6 Multiple pseudo-elements

Several pseudo elements can be combined:

```
P { color: red; font-size: 12pt }
P:first-letter { color: green; font-size: 200% }
P:first-line { color: blue }
```

```
<P>Some text that ends up on two lines</P>
```

In this example, the first letter of each 'P' element would be green with a font size of 24pt. The rest of the first line (as formatted on the canvas) would be blue while the rest of the paragraph would be red. Assuming that a line break will occur before the word "ends", the fictional tag sequence is:

```
<P>
<P:first-line>
<P:first-letter>
S
</P:first-letter>ome text that
</P:first-line>
ends up on two lines
</P>
```

Note that the 'first-letter' element is inside the 'first-line' element. Properties set on 'first-line' will be inherited by 'first-letter', but are overridden if the same property is set on 'first-letter'.

If a pseudo-element breaks up a real element the necessary extra tags must be regenerated in the fictional tag sequence. For example, if a SPAN element spans over a </P:first-line> tag, a set of SPAN end and start tags must be regenerated and the fictional tag sequence becomes:

```
<P>
<P:first-line>
<SPAN>
This text is inside a long
</SPAN>
</P:first-line>
<SPAN>
span element
</SPAN>
```

Chapter 3

The Cascade

In CSS, more than one style sheet can influence the presentation simultaneously. There are two main reasons for this feature: modularity and author/reader balance.

modularity

A style sheet designer can combine several (partial) style sheets to reduce redundancy:

```
@import url(http://www.style.org/pastoral);
@import url(http://www.style.org/marine);

H1 { color: red }       /* override imported sheets */
```

author/reader balance

Both readers and authors can influence the presentation through style sheets. To do so, they use the same style sheet language thus reflecting a fundamental feature of the web: everyone can become a publisher. The UA is free to choose the mechanism for referencing personal style sheets.

Sometimes conflicts will arise between the style sheets that influence the presentation. Conflict resolution is based on each style rule having a weight. By default, the weights of the reader's rules are less than the weights of rules in the author's documents. I.e., if there are conflicts between the style sheets of an incoming document and the reader's personal sheets, the author's rules will be used. Both reader and author rules override the UA's default values.

The imported style sheets also cascade with each other, in the order they are imported, according to the cascading rules defined below. Any rules specified in the style sheet itself override rules in imported style sheets. That is, imported style sheets are lower in the cascading order than rules in the style sheet itself. Imported style sheets can themselves import and override other style sheets, recursively.

In CSS1, all '@import' statements must occur at the start of a style sheet, before any declarations. This makes it easy to see that rules in the style sheet itself override rules in the imported style sheets.

3.1 'important'

Style sheet designers can increase the weights of their declarations:

```
H1 { color: black ! important; background: white ! important }
P  { font-size: 12pt ! important; font-style: italic }
```

In the example above, the first three declarations have increased weight, while the last declaration has normal weight.

A reader rule with an important declaration will override an author rule with a normal declaration. An author rule with an important declaration will override a reader rule with an important declaration.

3.2 Cascading order

Conflicting rules are intrinsic to the CSS mechanism. To find the value for an element/property combination, the following algorithm must be followed:

1. Find all declarations that apply to the element/property in question. Declarations apply if the selector matches the element in question. If no declarations apply, the inherited value is used. If there is no inherited value (this is the case for the 'HTML' element and for properties that do not inherit), the initial value is used.

2. Sort the declarations by explicit weight: declarations marked 'important' carry more weight than unmarked (normal) declarations.

3. Sort by origin: the author's style sheets override the reader's style sheet which override the UA's default values. An imported style sheet has the same origin as the style sheet from which it is imported.

4. Sort by specificity of selector: more specific selectors will override more general ones. To find the specificity, count the number of ID attributes in the selector (a), the number of CLASS attributes in the selector (b), and the number of tag names in the selector (c). Concatenating the three numbers (in a number system with a large base) gives the specificity. Some examples:

```
LI              {...}   /* a=0 b=0 c=1 -> specificity =   1 */
UL LI           {...}   /* a=0 b=0 c=2 -> specificity =   2 */
UL OL LI        {...}   /* a=0 b=0 c=3 -> specificity =   3 */
LI.red          {...}   /* a=0 b=1 c=1 -> specificity =  11 */
UL OL LI.red    {...}   /* a=0 b=1 c=3 -> specificity =  13 */
```

```
#x34y              {...}   /* a=1 b=0 c=0 -> specificity = 100 */
```
Pseudo-elements and pseudo-classes are counted as normal elements and classes, respectively.

5. Sort by order specified: if two rules have the same weight, the latter specified wins. Rules in imported style sheets are considered to be before any rules in the style sheet itself.

The search for the property value can be terminated whenever one rule has a higher weight than the other rules that apply to the same element/property combination.

This strategy gives author's style sheets considerably higher weight than those of the reader. It is therefore important that the reader has the ability to turn off the influence of a certain style sheet, e.g. through a pull-down menu.

A declaration in the 'STYLE' attribute of an element (see section 1.1 for an example) has the same weight as a declaration with an ID-based selector that is specified at the end of the style sheet:

```
<STYLE TYPE="text/css">
   #x97z { color: blue }
</STYLE>

<P ID=x97z STYLE="color: red">
```

In the above example, the color of the 'P' element would be red. Although the specificity is the same for both declarations, the declaration in the 'STYLE' attribute will override the one in the 'STYLE' element because of cascading rule number 5.

The UA may choose to honor other stylistic HTML attributes, for example 'ALIGN'. If so, these attributes are translated to the corresponding CSS rules with specificity equal to 1. The rules are assumed to be at the start of the author style sheet and may be overridden by subsequent style sheet rules. In a transition phase, this policy will make it easier for stylistic attributes to coexist with style sheets.

Chapter 4

Formatting Model

CSS1 assumes a simple box-oriented formatting model where each formatted element results in one or more rectangular boxes. (Elements that have a 'display' value of 'none' are not formatted and will therefore not result in a box.) All boxes have a core content area with optional surrounding padding, border and margin areas.

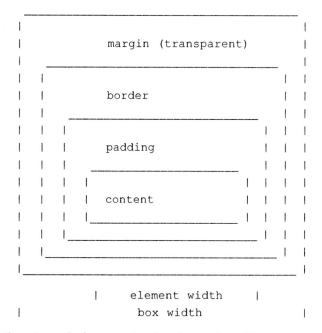

The size of the margin, border and padding are set with the margin (5.5.1–5.5.5), padding (5.5.6–5.5.10), and border (5.5.11–5.5.22) properties respectively. The padding area uses the same background as the element itself (set with the background properties (5.3.2–5.3.7)). The color and style for the border is set with the border properties. The margins are always transparent, so the parent element will shine through.

The size of the box is the sum of the element width (i.e. formatted text or image) and the padding, the border and the margin areas.

From the formatter's point of view there are two main types of elements: block-level and inline.

4.1 Block-level elements

Elements with a 'display' value of 'block' or 'list-item' are block-level elements. Also, floating elements (elements with a 'float' value other than 'none') are considered to be block-level elements.

The following example shows how margins and padding format a 'UL' element with two children. To simplify the diagram there are no borders. Also, the single-letter "constants" in this example are not legal CSS1 syntax, but is a convenient way to tie the style sheet values to the figure.

```
<STYLE TYPE="text/css">
  UL {
    background: red;
    margin: A B C D;
    padding: E F G H;
  }
  LI {
    color: white;
    background: blue;       /* so text is white on blue */
    margin: a b c d;
    padding: e f g h;
  }
</STYLE>
..
<UL>
  <LI>1st element of list
  <LI>2nd element of list
</UL>
```

```
 _____
|                                                      |
|      A         UL margin (transparent)               |
|     _____        |
| D  |                                         |  | B  |
|    |    E   UL padding (red)                  |  |    |
|    |    _____   |  |    |
|    | H |                                   |  | F|    |
|    |   |   a   LI margin (transparent,      |  |  |    |
|    |   |       so red shines through)       |  |  |    |
|    |   |    _____   |  |  |    |
|    |   | d |                            | b |  |  |    |
|    |   |   |   e    LI padding (blue)    |   |  |  |    |
|    |   |   |                            |   |  |  |    |
|    |   |   | h  1st element of list    f |   |  |  |    |
|    |   |   |                            |   |  |  |    |
|    |   |   |   g                        |   |  |  |    |
|    |   |   |_____|   |  |  |    |
|    |   |                                    |  |  |    |
|    |   |     max(a, c)                      |  |  | <- note the max
|    |   |    _____   |  |  |    |
|    |   | d |   e    LI padding (blue)    |   |  |  |    |
|    |   |   |                            |   |  |  |    |
|    |   |   | h  2nd element of list    f |   |  |  |    |
|    |   |   |                            |   |  |  |    |
|    |   |   |   g                        |   |  |  |    |
|    |   |   |_____|   |  |  |    |
|    |   |                                    |  |  |    |
|    |   |   c    LI margin (transparent,     |  |  |    |
|    |   |        so red shines through)      |  |  |    |
|    |   |_____    |  |  |    |
|    |                                         |  |    |
|    |    G                                    |  |    |
|    |_____|  |    |
|                                                  |    |
|      C                                           |    |
```

|_____ |

Technically, padding and margin properties are not inherited. But, as the example shows, the placement of an element is relative to ancestors and siblings, so these elements' padding and margin properties have an effect on their children.

If there had been borders in the above example they would have appeared between the padding and the margins.

The following diagram introduces some useful terminology:

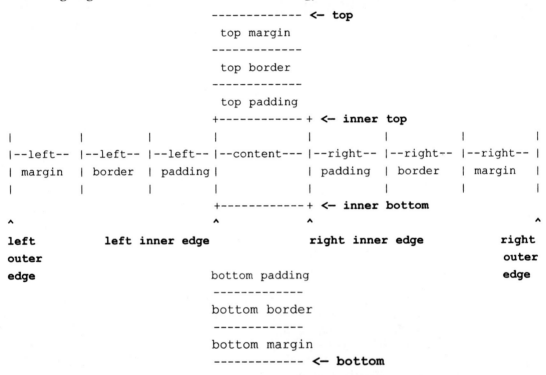

The *left outer edge* is the edge of an element with its padding, border and margin taken into account. The *left inner edge* is the edge of the content only, inside any padding, border or margin. Ditto for right. The *top* is the top of the element including any padding, border and margin; it is only defined for inline and floating elements, not for non-floating block-level elements. The *inner top* is the top of the content, inside any padding, border or margin. The *bottom* is the bottom of the element, outside any padding, border and margin; it is only defined for inline and floating elements, not for non-floating block-level elements. The *inner bottom* is the bottom of the element, inside any padding, border and margin.

The width of an element is the width of the content, i.e., the distance between left inner edge and right inner edge. The height is the height of the content, i.e., the distance from inner top to inner bottom.

4.1.1 Vertical formatting

The width of the margin on non-floating block-level elements specifies the minimum distance to the edges of surrounding boxes. Two or more adjoining vertical margins (i.e., with no border, padding or content between them) are collapsed to use the maximum of the margin values. In most cases, after collapsing the vertical margins the result is visually more pleasing and closer to what the designer expects. In the example above, the margins between the two 'LI' elements are collapsed by using the maximum of the first LI element's 'margin-bottom' and the second LI element's 'margin-top'. Similarly, if the padding between the 'UL' and the first 'LI' element (the "E" constant) had been zero, the margins of the UL and first LI elements would have been collapsed.

In the case of negative margins, the absolute maximum of the negative adjoining margins is deducted from the maximum of the positive adjoining margins. If there are no positive margins, the absolute maximum of the negative adjoining margins is deducted from zero.

4.1.2 Horizontal formatting

The horizontal position and size of a non-floating, block-level element is determined by seven properties: 'margin-left', 'border-left', 'padding-left', 'width', 'padding-right', 'border-right' and 'margin-right'. The sum of these seven is always equal to the 'width' of the parent element.

By default, the 'width' of an element is 'auto'. If the element is not a replaced element, this means that the 'width' is calculated by the UA so that the sum of the seven properties mentioned above is equal to the parent width. If the element is a replaced element, a value of 'auto' for 'width' is automatically replaced by the element's intrinsic width.

Three of the seven properties can be set to 'auto': 'margin-left', 'width' and 'margin-right'. For replaced elements, a value of 'auto' on 'width' is replaced by the intrinsic width, so for them there can only be two 'auto' values.

The 'width' has a non-negative UA-defined minimum value (which may vary from element to element and even depend on other properties). If 'width' goes below this limit, either because it was set explicitly, or because it was 'auto' and the rules below would make it too small, the value will be replaced with the minimum value instead.

If *exactly one* of 'margin-left', 'width' or 'margin-right' is 'auto', the UA will assign that property a value that will make the sum of the seven equal to the parent's width.

If *none* of the properties are 'auto', the value of 'margin-right' will be assigned 'auto'.

If *more than one* of the three is 'auto', and one of them is 'width', then the others ('margin-left' and/or 'margin-right') will be set to zero and 'width' will get the value needed to make the sum of the seven equal to the parent's width.

Otherwise, if both 'margin-left' and 'margin-right' are 'auto', they will be set to equal values. This will center the element inside its parent.

If 'auto' is set as the value for one of the seven properties in an element that is inline or floating, it will be treated as if it were set to zero.

Unlike vertical margins, horizontal margins are not collapsed.

4.1.3 List-item elements

Elements with a 'display' property value of 'list-item' are formatted as block-level elements, but preceded by a list-item marker. The type of marker is determined by the 'list-style' property. The marker is placed according to the value of the 'list-style' property:

```
<STYLE TYPE="text/css">
   UL            { list-style: outside }
   UL.compact { list-style: inside }
</STYLE>

<UL>
   <LI>first list item comes first
   <LI>second list item comes second
</UL>

<UL CLASS=COMPACT>
   <LI>first list item comes first
   <LI>second list item comes second
</UL>
```

The above example may be formatted as:

```
* first list item
  comes first

* second list item
```

```
   comes second

*  first list
   item comes first

   *  second list
   item comes second
```

In right-to-left text, the markers would have been on the right side of the box.

4.1.4 Floating elements

Using the 'float' property, an element can be declared to be outside the normal flow of elements and is then formatted as a block-level element. For example, by setting the 'float' property of an image to 'left', the image is moved to the left until the margin, padding or border of another block-level element is reached. The normal flow will wrap around on the right side. The margins, borders and padding of the element itself will be honored, and the margins never collapse with the margins of adjacent elements.

A floating element is positioned subject to the following constraints (see section 4.1 for an explanation of the terms):

1. The left outer edge of a left-floating element may not be to the left of the left inner edge of its parent element. Analogously for right floating elements.

2. The left outer edge of a left floating element must be to the right of the right outer edge of every earlier (in the HTML source) left-floating element or the top of the former must be lower than the bottom of the latter. Analogously for right floating elements.

3. The right outer edge of a left-floating element may not be to the right of the left outer edge of any right-floating element that is to the right of it. Analogously for right-floating elements.

4. A floating element's top may not be higher than the inner top of its parent.

5. A floating element's top may not be higher than the top of any earlier floating or block-level element.

6. A floating element's top may not be higher than the top of any line-box (see section 4.4) with content that precedes the floating element in the HTML source.

7. A floating element must be placed as high as possible.

8. A left-floating element must be put as far to the left as possible, a right-floating element as far to the right as possible. A higher position is preferred over one that is further to the left/right.

```
<STYLE TYPE="text/css">
  IMG { float: left }
  BODY, P, IMG { margin: 2em }
</STYLE>

<BODY>
  <P>
    <IMG SRC=img.gif>
    Some sample text that has no other...
</BODY>
```

The above example could be formatted as:

```
 _____
|
|             max(BODY margin, P margin)
|
|              _____
|    |    |                      Some sample text
| B  | P  | IMG margins that has no other
| O  |    |      _____        purpose than to
| D  | m  |     |      |        show how floating
| Y  | a  |     | IMG  |        elements are moved
|    | r  |     |      |        to the side of the
| m  | g  |     |_____|        parent element
| a  | i  |                     while honoring
| r  | n  |                     margins, borders
| g  |    |                     and padding. Note
| i  |    | how adjacent vertical margins
| n  |    | are collapsed between non-
|    |    | floating block-level elements.
```

Note that the margin of the 'P' element encloses the floating 'IMG' element.

There are two situations when floating elements can overlap with the margin, border and padding areas of other elements:

when the floating element has a negative margin: negative margins on floating elements are honored as on other block-level elements.

when the floating element is wider or higher than the element it is inside

4.2 Inline elements

Elements that are not formatted as block-level elements are inline elements. An inline element can share line space with other elements. Consider this example:

```
<P>Several <EM>emphasized</EM> words <STRONG>appear</STRONG>.</P>
```

The 'P' element is normally block-level, while 'EM' and 'STRONG' are inline elements. If the 'P' element is wide enough to format the whole element on one line, there will be two inline elements on the line:

```
Several emphasized words appear.
```

If there is not enough room on one line an inline element will be split into several boxes:

```
<P>Several <EM>emphasized words</EM> appear here.</P>
```

The above example may be formatted as:

```
Several emphasized
words appear here.
```

If the inline element has margins, borders, padding or text decorations attached, these will have no effect where the element is broken:

```
        -----------
Several |emphasized
        -----------

-----
words| appear here.
-----
```

(The "figure" above is slightly distorted due to the use of ASCII graphics. See section 4.4 for a description of how to calculate the height of lines.

4.3 Replaced elements

A replaced element is an element which is replaced by content pointed to from the element. E.g., in HTML, the 'IMG' element is replaced by the image pointed to by the 'SRC' attribute. One can assume that replaced elements come with their own intrinsic dimensions. If the value of the 'width' property is 'auto', the intrinsic width is used as the width of the element. If a value other than 'auto' is specified in the style sheet, this value is used and the replaced element is resized accordingly (the resize method will depend on the media type). The 'height' property is used in the same manner.

Replaced elements can be either block-level or inline.

4.4 The height of lines

All elements have a 'line-height' property that, in principle, gives the total height of a line of text. Space is added above and below the text of the line to arrive at that line height. For example, if the text is 12pt high and 'line-height' is set to '14pt', an extra space of 2pt is added, namely 1pt above and 1pt below the line. Empty elements influence these calculations just like elements with content.

The difference between the font size and the 'line-height' is called the leading. Half the leading is called the half-leading. After formatting, each line will form a rectangular line-box.

If a line of text contains sections with different 'line-height' values (because there are inline elements on the line), then each of those sections has its own half-leading above and below. The height of the line-box is from the top of the highest section to the bottom of the lowest one. Note that the top and bottom do not necessarily correspond to the tallest element, since elements can be positioned vertically with the 'vertical-align' property. To form a paragraph, each line-box is stacked immediately below the previous line.

Note that any padding, border or margin above and below non-replaced inline elements does not influence the height of the line. In other words: if the 'line-height' is too small for the chosen padding or border, it will overlap with text on other lines.

Replaced elements (e.g. images) on the line can make the line-box bigger, if the top of the replaced element (i.e., including all of its padding, border and margin) is above the tallest text section, or if the bottom is below the lowest.

In the normal case, when there is only one value of 'line-height' throughout a paragraph, and no tall images, the definition above will ensure that baselines of successive lines are exactly 'line-height' apart. This is important when columns of text in different fonts have to be aligned, for example in a table.

Note that this doesn't preclude the text on two adjacent lines from overlapping each other. The 'line-height' may be smaller than the height of the text, in which case the leading will be negative. This is useful if you know that the text will contain no descenders (e.g., because it only contains uppercase), so the lines can be put closer together.

4.5 The canvas

The canvas is the part of the UA's drawing surface onto which documents are rendered. No structural element of a document corresponds to the canvas, and this raises two issues when formatting a document:

- from where should the dimensions of the canvas be set?

- when the document doesn't cover the whole canvas, how should this area be rendered?

A reasonable answer to the first question is that the initial width of the canvas is based on the window size, but CSS1 leaves this issue for the UA to decide. It is also reasonable to expect the UA to change the width of the canvas when the window is resized, but this is also outside the scope of CSS1.

HTML extensions have set a precedent for the second question: attributes on the 'BODY' element set the background of the whole canvas. To support designers' expectations, CSS1 introduces a special rule to find the canvas background:

If the 'background' value of the 'HTML' element is different from 'transparent' then use it, else use the 'background' value of the 'BODY' element. If the resulting value is 'transparent', the rendering is undefined.

This rule allows:

```
<HTML STYLE="background: url(http://style.com/marble.png)">
<BODY STYLE="background: red">
```

In the example above, the canvas will be covered with "marble". The background of the 'BODY' element (which may or may not fully cover the canvas) will be red.

Until other means of addressing the canvas become available, it is recommended that canvas properties are set on the 'BODY' element.

4.6 'BR' elements

The current CSS1 properties and values cannot describe the behavior of the 'BR' element. In HTML, the 'BR' element specifies a line break between words. In effect, the element is replaced by a line break. Future versions of CSS may handle added and replaced content, but CSS1-based formatters must treat 'BR' specially.

Chapter 5

CSS1 Properties

Style sheets influence the presentation of documents by assigning values to style properties. This section lists the defined style properties, and their corresponding list of possible values, of CSS1.

5.1 Notation for property values

In the text below, the allowed values for each property are listed with a syntax like the following:

Value: N | NW | NE
Value: [<length> | thick | thin]{1,4}
Value: [<family-name> ,]* <family-name>
Value: <url>? <color> [/ <color>]?
Value: <url> || <color>

The words between "<" and ">" give a type of value. The most common types are <length>, <percentage>, <url>, <number> and <color>; these are described in section 6. The more specialized types (e.g. <font-family> and <border-style>) are described under the corresponding property.

Other words are keywords that must appear literally, without quotes. The slash (/) and the comma (,) must also appear literally.

Several things juxtaposed mean that all of them must occur, in the given order. A bar (|) separates alternatives: one of them must occur. A double bar (A || B) means that either A or B or both must occur, in any order. Brackets ([]) are for grouping. Juxtaposition is stronger than the double bar, and the double bar is stronger than the bar. Thus "a b | c || d e" is equivalent to "[a b] || [c | [d e]]".

Every type, keyword, or bracketed group may be followed by one of the following modifiers:

- An asterisk (*) indicates that the preceding type, word or group is repeated zero or more times.

- A plus (+) indicates that the preceding type, word or group is repeated one or more times.

- A question mark (?) indicates that the preceding type, word or group is optional.

- A pair of numbers in curly braces ({A,B}) indicates that the preceding type, word or group is repeated at least A and at most B times.

5.2 Font properties

Setting font properties will be among the most common uses of style sheets. Unfortunately, there exists no well-defined and universally accepted taxonomy for classifying fonts, and terms that apply to one font family may not be appropriate for others. E.g. 'italic' is commonly used to label slanted text, but slanted text may also be labeled as being *Oblique, Slanted, Incline, Cursive* or *Kursiv*. Therefore it is not a simple problem to map typical font selection properties to a specific font.

CSS1 defines the properties 'font-family', 'font-style', 'font-variant' and 'font-weight', 'font-size', 'font'.

5.2.1 Font matching

Because there is no accepted, universal taxonomy of font properties, matching of properties to font faces must be done carefully. The properties are matched in a well-defined order to insure that the results of this matching process are as consistent as possible across UAs (assuming that the same library of font faces is presented to each of them).

1. The User Agent makes (or accesses) a database of relevant CSS1 properties of all the fonts of which the UA is aware. The UA may be aware of a font because it has been installed locally or it has been previously downloaded over the web. If there are two fonts with exactly the same properties, one of them is ignored.

2. At a given element and for each character in that element, the UA assembles the font-properties applicable to that element. Using the complete set of properties, the UA uses the 'font-family' property to choose a tentative font family. The remaining properties are tested against the family according to the matching criteria described with each property. If there are matches for all the remaining properties, then that is the matching font face for the given element.

3. If there is no matching font face within the 'font-family' being processed by step 2, and if there is a next alternative 'font-family' in the font set, then repeat step 2 with the next alternative 'font-family'.

4. If there is a matching font face, but it doesn't contain a glyph for the current character, and if there is a next alternative 'font-family' in the font sets, then repeat step 2 with the next alternative 'font-family'. See appendix C for a description of font and character encoding.

5. If there is no font within the family selected in 2, then use a UA-dependent default 'font-family' and repeat step 2, using the best match that can be obtained within the default font.

(The above algorithm can be optimized to avoid having to revisit the CSS1 properties for each character.)

The per-property matching rules from (2) above are as follows:

1. 'font-style' is tried first. 'italic' will be satisfied if there is either a face in the UA's font database labeled with the CSS keyword 'italic' (preferred) or 'oblique'. Otherwise the values must be matched exactly or font-style will fail.

2. 'font-variant' is tried next. 'normal' matches a font not labeled as 'small-caps'; 'small-caps' matches (1) a font labeled as 'small-caps', (2) a font in which the small caps are synthesized, or (3) a font where all lowercase letters are replaced by upper case letters. A small-caps font may be synthesized by electronically scaling uppercase letters from a normal font.

3. 'font-weight' is matched next, it will never fail. (See 'font-weight' below.)

4. 'font-size' must be matched within a UA-dependent margin of tolerance. (Typically, sizes for scalable fonts are rounded to the nearest whole pixel, while the tolerance for bitmapped fonts could be as large as 20%.) Further computations, e.g. by 'em' values in other properties, are based on the 'font-size' value that is used, not the one that is specified.

5.2.2 'font-family'

Value: [[<family-name> | <generic-family>],]* [<family-name> | <generic-family>]
Initial: UA specific
Applies to: all elements
Inherited: yes
Percentage values: N/A

The value is a prioritized list of font family names and/or generic family names. Unlike most other CSS1 properties, values are separated by a comma to indicate that they are alternatives:

```
BODY { font-family: gill, helvetica, sans-serif }
```

There are two types of list values:

41

<family-name>

The name of a font family of choice. In the last example, "gill" and "helvetica" are font families.

<generic-family>

In the example above, the last value is a generic family name. The following generic families are defined:

- 'serif' (e.g. Times)

- 'sans-serif' (e.g. Helvetica)

- 'cursive' (e.g. Zapf-Chancery)

- 'fantasy' (e.g. Western)

- 'monospace' (e.g. Courier)

Style sheet designers are encouraged to offer a generic font family as a last alternative.

Font names containing whitespace should be quoted:

```
BODY { font-family: "new century schoolbook", serif }

<BODY STYLE="font-family: 'My own font', fantasy">
```

If quoting is omitted, any whitespace characters before and after the font name are ignored and any sequence of whitespace characters inside the font name is converted to a single space.

5.2.3 'font-style'

Value: normal | italic | oblique
Initial: normal
Applies to: all elements
Inherited: yes
Percentage values: N/A

The 'font-style' property selects between normal (sometimes referred to as "roman" or "upright"), italic and oblique faces within a font family.

A value of 'normal' selects a font that is classified as 'normal' in the UA's font database, while 'oblique' selects a font that is labeled 'oblique'. A value of 'italic' selects a font that is labeled 'italic', or, if that is not available, one labeled 'oblique'.

The font that is labeled 'oblique' in the UA's font database may actually have been generated by electronically slanting a normal font.

Fonts with Oblique, Slanted or Incline in their names will typically be labeled 'oblique' in the UA's font database. Fonts with Italic, Cursive or Kursiv in their names will typically be labeled 'italic'.

```
H1, H2, H3 { font-style: italic }
H1 EM { font-style: normal }
```

In the example above, emphasized text within 'H1' will appear in a normal face.

5.2.4 'font-variant'

Value: normal | small-caps
Initial: normal
Applies to: all elements
Inherited: yes
Percentage values: N/A

Another type of variation within a font family is the small-caps. In a small-caps font the lower case letters look similar to the uppercase ones, but in a smaller size and with slightly different proportions. The 'font-variant' property selects that font.

A value of 'normal' selects a font that is not a small-caps font, 'small-caps' selects a small-caps font. It is acceptable (but not required) in CSS1 if the small-caps font is a created by taking a normal font and replacing the lower case letters by scaled uppercase characters. As a last resort, uppercase letters will be used as replacement for a small-caps font.

The following example results in an 'H3' element in small-caps, with emphasized words in oblique small-caps:

```
H3 { font-variant: small-caps }
EM { font-style: oblique }
```

There may be other variants in the font family as well, such as fonts with old-style numerals, small-caps numerals, condensed or expanded letters, etc. CSS1 has no properties that select those.

CSS1 core: insofar as this property causes text to be transformed to uppercase, the same considerations as for 'text-transform' apply.

5.2.5 'font-weight'

Value: normal | bold | bolder | lighter | 100 | 200 | 300 | 400 | 500 | 600 | 700 | 800 | 900
Initial: normal
Applies to: all elements
Inherited: yes
Percentage values: N/A

The 'font-weight' property selects the weight of the font. The values '100' to '900' form an ordered sequence, where each number indicates a weight that is at least as dark as its predecessor. The keyword 'normal' is synonymous with '400', and 'bold' is synonymous with '700'. Keywords other than 'normal' and 'bold' have been shown to be often confused with font names and a numerical scale was therefore chosen for the 9-value list.

```
P { font-weight: normal }    /* 400 */
H1 { font-weight: 700 }      /* bold */
```

The 'bolder' and 'lighter' values select font weights that are relative to the weight inherited from the parent:

```
STRONG { font-weight: bolder }
```

Child elements inherit the resultant weight, not the keyword value.

Fonts (the font data) typically have one or more properties whose values are names that are descriptive of the "weight" of a font. There is no accepted, universal meaning to these weight names. Their primary role is to distinguish faces of differing darkness within a single font family. Usage across font families is quite variant; for example a font that you might think of as being bold might be described as being *Regular, Roman, Book, Medium, Semi-* or *DemiBold, Bold,* or *Black,* depending on how black the "normal" face of the font is within the design. Because there is no standard usage of names, the weight property values in CSS1 are given on a numerical scale in which the value '400' (or 'normal') corresponds to the "normal" text face for that family. The weight name associated with that face will typically be *Book, Regular, Roman, Normal* or sometimes *Medium*.

The association of other weights within a family to the numerical weight values is intended only to preserve the ordering of darkness within that family. However, the following heuristics tell how the assignment is done in typical cases:

- If the font family already uses a numerical scale with nine values (like e.g. *OpenType* does), the font weights should be mapped directly.

- If there is both a face labeled *Medium* and one labeled *Book, Regular, Roman* or *Normal,* then the *Medium* is normally assigned to the '500'.

- The font labeled "Bold" will often correspond to the weight value '700'.

- If there are fewer then 9 weights in the family, the default algorithm for filling the "holes" is as follows. If '500' is unassigned, it will be assigned the same font as '400'. If any of the values '600', '700', '800' or '900' remains unassigned, they are assigned to the same face as the next darker assigned keyword, if any, or the next lighter one otherwise. If any of '300', '200' or '100' remains unassigned, it is assigned to the next lighter assigned keyword, if any, or the next darker otherwise.

The following two examples illustrate the process. Assume four weights in the "Example1" family, from lightest to darkest: *Regular, Medium, Bold, Heavy*. And assume six weights in the "Example2" family: *Book, Medium, Bold, Heavy, Black, ExtraBlack*. Note how in the second example it has been decided not to assign "Example2 ExtraBlack" to anything.

Available faces	Assignments	Filling the holes
"Example1 Regular"	400	100, 200, 300
"Example1 Medium"	500	
"Example1 Bold"	700	600
"Example1 Heavy"	800	900
Available faces	Assignments	Filling the holes
"Example2 Book"	400	100, 200, 300
"Example2 Medium"	500	
"Example2 Bold"	700	600
"Example2 Heavy"	800	
"Example2 Black"	900	
"Example2 ExtraBlack"	(none)	

Since the intent of the relative keywords 'bolder' and 'lighter' is to darken or lighten the face *within the family* and because a family may not have faces aligned with all the symbolic weight values, the matching of 'bolder' is to the next darker face available on the client within the family and the matching of 'lighter' is to the next lighter face within the family. To be precise, the meaning of the relative keywords 'bolder' and 'lighter' is as follows:

- 'bolder' selects the next weight that is assigned to a font that is darker than the inherited one. If there is no such weight, it simply results in the next darker numerical value (and the font remains unchanged), unless the inherited value was '900' in which case the resulting weight is also '900'.

- 'lighter' is similar, but works in the opposite direction: it selects the next lighter keyword with a different font from the inherited one, unless there is no such font, in which case it selects the next lighter numerical value (and keeps the font unchanged).

There is no guarantee that there will be a darker face for each of the 'font-weight' values; for example, some fonts may have only a normal and a bold face, others may have eight different face weights. There is no guarantee on how a UA will map font faces within a family to weight values. The only guarantee is that a face of a given value will be no less dark than the faces of lighter values.

5.2.6 'font-size'

Value: <absolute-size> | <relative-size> | <length> | <percentage>
Initial: medium
Applies to: all elements
Inherited: yes
Percentage values: relative to parent element's font size

<absolute-size>

An <absolute-size> keyword is an index to a table of font sizes computed and kept by the UA. Possible values are: [xx-small | x-small | small | medium | large | x-large | xx-large]. On a computer screen a scaling factor of 1.5 is suggested between adjacent indexes; if the 'medium' font is 10pt, the 'large' font could be 15pt. Different media may need different scaling factors. Also, the UA should take the quality and availability of fonts into account when computing the table. The table may be different from one font family to another.

<relative-size>

A <relative-size> keyword is interpreted relative to the table of font sizes and the font size of the parent element. Possible values are: [larger | smaller]. For example, if the parent element has a font size of 'medium', a value of 'larger' will make the font size of the current element be 'large'. If the parent element's size is not close to a table entry, the UA is free to interpolate between table entries or round off to the closest one. The UA may have to extrapolate table values if the numerical value goes beyond the keywords.

Length and percentage values should not take the font size table into account when calculating the font size of the element.

Negative values are not allowed.

On all other properties, 'em' and 'ex' length values refer to the font size of the current element. On the 'font-size' property, these length units refer to the font size of the parent element.

Note that an application may reinterpret an explicit size, depending on the context. E.g., inside a VR scene a font may get a different size because of perspective distortion.

Examples:

```
P { font-size: 12pt; }
BLOCKQUOTE { font-size: larger }
EM { font-size: 150% }
EM { font-size: 1.5em }
```

If the suggested scaling factor of 1.5 is used, the last three declarations are identical.

5.2.7 'font'

Value: [<font-style> || <font-variant> || <font-weight>]? <font-size> [/ <line-height>]? <font-family>
Initial: not defined for shorthand properties
Applies to: all elements
Inherited: yes
Percentage values: allowed on <font-size> and <line-height>

The 'font' property is a shorthand property for setting 'font-style' 'font-variant' 'font-weight' 'font-size', 'line-height' and 'font-family' at the same place in the style sheet. The syntax of this property is based on a traditional typographical shorthand notation to set multiple properties related to fonts.

For a definition of allowed and initial values, see the previously defined properties. Properties for which no values are given are set to their initial value.

```
P { font: 12pt/14pt sans-serif }
P { font: 80% sans-serif }
P { font: x-large/110% "new century schoolbook", serif }
P { font: bold italic large Palatino, serif }
P { font: normal small-caps 120%/120% fantasy }
```

In the second rule, the font size percentage value ('80%') refers to the font size of the parent element. In the third rule, the line height percentage refers to the font size of the element itself.

In the first three rules above, the 'font-style', 'font-variant' and 'font-weight' are not explicitly mentioned, which means they are all three set to their initial value ('normal'). The fourth rule sets the 'font-weight' to 'bold', the 'font-style' to 'italic' and implicitly sets 'font-variant' to 'normal'.

The fifth rule sets the 'font-variant' ('small-caps'), the 'font-size' (120% of the parent's font), the 'line-height' (120% times the font size) and the 'font-family' ('fantasy'). It follows that the keyword 'normal' applies to the two remaining properties: 'font-style' and 'font-weight'.

5.3 Color and background properties

These properties describe the color (often *called foreground color*) and background of an element (i.e. the surface onto which the content is rendered). One can set a background color and/or a background image. The position of the image, if/how it is repeated, and whether it is fixed or scrolled relative to the canvas can also be set.

The 'color' property inherits normally. The background properties do not inherit, but the parent element's background will shine through by default because of the initial 'transparent' value on 'background-color'.

5.3.1 'color'

Value: <color>
Initial: UA specific
Applies to: all elements
Inherited: yes
Percentage values: N/A

This property describes the text color of an element (often referred to as the foreground color). There are different ways to specify red:

```
EM { color: red }                /* natural language */
EM { color: rgb(255,0,0) }       /* RGB range 0-255    */
```

See section 6.3 for a description of possible color values.

5.3.2 'background-color'

Value: <color> | transparent
Initial: transparent
Applies to: all elements
Inherited: no
Percentage values: N/A

This property sets the background color of an element.

```
H1 { background-color: #F00 }
```

5.3.3 'background-image'

Value: <url> | none
Initial: none
Applies to: all elements
Inherited: no
Percentage values: N/A

This property sets the background image of an element. When setting a background image, one should also set a background color that will be used when the image is unavailable. When the image is available, it is overlaid on top of the background color.

```
BODY { background-image: url(marble.gif) }
P { background-image: none }
```

5.3.4 'background-repeat'

Value: repeat | repeat-x | repeat-y | no-repeat
Initial: repeat
Applies to: all elements
Inherited: no
Percentage values: N/A

If a background image is specified, the value of 'background-repeat' determines how/if the image is repeated.

A value of 'repeat' means that the image is repeated both horizontally and vertically. The 'repeat-x' ('repeat-y') value makes the image repeat horizontally (vertically), to create a single band of images from one side to the other. With a value of 'no-repeat', the image is not repeated.

```
BODY {
   background: red url(pendant.gif);
   background-repeat: repeat-y;
}
```

In the example above, the image will only be repeated vertically.

5.3.5 'background-attachment'

Value: scroll | fixed
Initial: scroll
Applies to: all elements
Inherited: no
Percentage values: N/A

If a background image is specified, the value of 'background-attachment' determines if it is fixed with regard to the canvas or if it scrolls along with the content.

```
BODY {
    background: red url(pendant.gif);
    background-repeat: repeat-y;
    background-attachment: fixed;
}
```

CSS1 core: UAs may treat 'fixed' as 'scroll'. However, it is recommended they interpret 'fixed' correctly, at least on the HTML and BODY elements, since there is no way for an author to provide an image only for those browsers that support 'fixed'. (See section 7.)

5.3.6 'background-position'

Value: [<percentage> | <length>]{1,2} | [top | center | bottom] || [left | center | right]
Initial: 0% 0%
Applies to: block-level and replaced elements
Inherited: no
Percentage values: refer to the size of the element itself

If a background image has been specified, the value of 'background-position' specifies its initial position.

With a value pair of '0% 0%', the upper left corner of the image is placed in the upper left corner of the box that surrounds the content of the element (i.e., not the box that surrounds the padding, border or margin). A value pair of '100% 100%' places the lower right corner of the image in the lower right corner of the element. With a value pair of '14% 84%', the point 14% across and 84% down the image is to be placed at the point 14% across and 84% down the element.

With a value pair of '2cm 2cm', the upper left corner of the image is placed 2cm to the right and 2cm below the upper left corner of the element.

If only one percentage or length value is given, it sets the horizontal position only, the vertical position will be 50%. If two values are given, the horizontal position comes first. Combinations of length and percentage values are allowed, e.g. '50% 2cm'. Negative positions are allowed.

One can also use keyword values to indicate the position of the background image. Keywords cannot be combined with percentage values, or length values. The possible combinations of keywords and their interpretations are as follows:

- 'top left' and 'left top' both mean the same as '0% 0%'.

- 'top', 'top center' and 'center top' mean the same as '50% 0%'.

- 'right top' and 'top right' mean the same as '100% 0%'.

- 'left', 'left center' and 'center left' mean the same as '0% 50%'.

- 'center' and 'center center' mean the same as '50% 50%'.

- 'right', 'right center' and 'center right' mean the same as '100% 50%'.

- 'bottom left' and 'left bottom' mean the same as '0% 100%'.

- 'bottom', 'bottom center' and 'center bottom' mean the same as '50% 100%'.

- 'bottom right' and 'right bottom' mean the same as '100% 100%'.

Examples:

```
BODY { background: url(banner.jpeg) right top }    /* 100%    0% */
BODY { background: url(banner.jpeg) top center }   /*  50%    0% */
BODY { background: url(banner.jpeg) center }       /*  50%   50% */
BODY { background: url(banner.jpeg) bottom }       /*  50%  100% */
```

If the background image is fixed with regard to the canvas (see the 'background-attachment' property above), the image is placed relative to the canvas instead of the element. E.g.:

```
BODY {
   background-image: url(logo.png);
   background-attachment: fixed;
   background-position: 100% 100%;
}
```

In the example above, the image is placed in the lower right corner of the canvas.

5.3.7 'background'

Value: <background-color> || <background-image> || <background-repeat> || <background-attachment> || <background-position>
Initial: not defined for shorthand properties
Applies to: all elements
Inherited: no
Percentage values: allowed on <background-position>

The 'background' property is a shorthand property for setting the individual background properties (i.e., 'background-color', 'background-image', 'background-repeat', 'background-attachment' and 'background-position') at the same place in the style sheet.

Possible values on the 'background' properties are the set of all possible values on the individual properties.

```
BODY { background: red }
P { background: url(chess.png) gray 50% repeat fixed }
```

The 'background' property always sets all the individual background properties. In the first rule of the above example, only a value for 'background-color' has been given and the other individual properties are set to their initial value. In the second rule, all individual properties have been specified.

5.4 Text properties

5.4.1 'word-spacing'

Value: normal | <length>
Initial: normal
Applies to: all elements
Inherited: yes
Percentage values: N/A

The length unit indicates an addition to the default space between words. Values can be negative, but there may be implementation-specific limits. The UA is free to select the exact spacing algorithm. The word spacing may also be influenced by justification (which is a value of the 'text-align' property).

```
H1 { word-spacing: 1em }
```

Here, the word-spacing between each word in 'H1' elements would be increased by '1em'.

CSS1 core: UAs may interpret any value of 'word-spacing' as 'normal'. (See section 7.)

5.4.2 'letter-spacing'

Value: normal | <length>
Initial: normal
Applies to: all elements
Inherited: yes
Percentage values: N/A

The length unit indicates an addition to the default space between characters. Values can be negative, but there may be implementation-specific limits. The UA is free to select the exact spacing algorithm. The letter spacing may also be influenced by justification (which is a value of the 'align' property).

```
BLOCKQUOTE { letter-spacing: 0.1em }
```

Here, the letter-spacing between each character in 'BLOCKQUOTE' elements would be increased by '0.1em'.

With a value of 'normal', the UAs may change the space between letters to justify text. This will not happen if 'letter-spacing' is explicitly set to a <length> value:

```
BLOCKQUOTE { letter-spacing: 0 }
BLOCKQUOTE { letter-spacing: 0cm }
```

When the resultant space between two letters is not the same as the default space, UAs should not use ligatures.

CSS1 core: UAs may interpret any value of 'letter-spacing' as 'normal'. (See section 7.)

5.4.3 'text-decoration'

Value: none | [underline || overline || line-through || blink]
Initial: none
Applies to: all elements
Inherited: no, but see clarification below
Percentage values: N/A

This property describes decorations that are added to the text of an element. If the element has no text (e.g. the 'IMG' element in HTML) or is an empty element (e.g. '<EM></EM>'), this property has no effect. A value of 'blink' causes the text to blink.

The color(s) required for the text decoration should be derived from the 'color' property value.

This property is not inherited, but elements should match their parent. E.g., if an element is underlined, the line should span the child elements. The color of the underlining will remain the same even if descendant elements have different 'color' values.

```
A:link, A:visited, A:active { text-decoration: underline }
```

The example above would underline the text of all links (i.e., all 'A' elements with a 'HREF' attribute).

UAs must recognize the keyword 'blink', but are not required to support the blink effect.

5.4.4 'vertical-align'

Value: baseline | sub | super | top | text-top | middle | bottom | text-bottom | <percentage>
Initial: baseline
Applies to: inline elements
Inherited: no
Percentage values: refer to the 'line-height' of the element itself

The property affects the vertical positioning of the element. One set of keywords is relative to the parent element:

'baseline'

align the baseline of the element (or the bottom, if the element doesn't have a baseline) with the baseline of the parent

'middle'

align the vertical midpoint of the element (typically an image) with the baseline plus half the x-height of the parent

'sub'

subscript the element

'super'

superscript the element

'text-top'

align the top of the element with the top of the parent element's font

'text-bottom'

align the bottom of the element with the bottom of the parent element's font

Another set of properties are relative to the formatted line that the element is a part of:

'top'

    align the top of the element with the tallest element on the line

'bottom'

    align the bottom of the element with the lowest element on the line

Using the 'top' and 'bottom' alignment, unsolvable situations can occur where element dependencies form a loop.

Percentage values refer to the value of the 'line-height' property of the element itself. They raise the baseline of the element (or the bottom, if it has no baseline) the specified amount above the baseline of the parent. Negative values are possible. E.g., a value of '-100%' will lower the element so that the baseline of the element ends up where the baseline of the next line should have been. This allows precise control over the vertical position of elements (such as images that are used in place of letters) that don't have a baseline.

It is expected that a future version of CSS will allow <length> as a value on this property.

5.4.5 'text-transform'

Value: capitalize | uppercase | lowercase | none
Initial: none
Applies to: all elements
Inherited: yes
Percentage values: N/A

'capitalize'

    uppercases the first character of each word

'uppercase'

    uppercases all letters of the element

'lowercase'

    lowercases all letters of the element

'none'

    neutralizes inherited value.

The actual transformation in each case is human language dependent. See [4] for ways to find the language of an element.

```
H1 { text-transform: uppercase }
```

The example above would put 'H1' elements in uppercase text.

CSS1 core: UAs may ignore 'text-transform' (i.e., treat it as 'none') for characters that are not from the Latin-1 repertoire and for elements in languages for which the transformation is different from that specified by the case-conversion tables of Unicode [8].

5.4.6 'text-align'

Value: left | right | center | justify
Initial: UA specific
Applies to: block-level elements
Inherited: yes
Percentage values: N/A

This property describes how text is aligned within the element. The actual justification algorithm used is UA and human language dependent.

Example:

```
DIV.center { text-align: center }
```

Since 'text-align' inherits, all block-level elements inside the 'DIV' element with 'CLASS=center' will be centered. Note that alignments are relative to the width of the element, not the canvas. If 'justify' is not supported, the UA will supply a replacement. Typically, this will be 'left' for western languages.

CSS1 core: UAs may treat 'justify' as 'left' or 'right', depending on whether the element's default writing direction is left-to-right or right-to-left, respectively.

5.4.7 'text-indent'

Value: <length> | <percentage>
Initial: 0
Applies to: block-level elements
Inherited: yes
Percentage values: refer to parent element's width

The property specifies the indentation that appears before the first formatted line. The value of 'text-indent' may be negative, but there may be implementation-specific limits. An indentation is not inserted in the middle of an element that was broken by another (such as 'BR' in HTML).

Example:

```
P { text-indent: 3em }
```

5.4.8 'line-height'

Value: normal | <number> | <length> | <percentage>
Initial: normal
Applies to: all elements
Inherited: yes
Percentage values: relative to the font size of the element itself

The property sets the distance between two adjacent lines' baselines.

When a numerical value is specified, the line height is given by the font size of the current element multiplied with the numerical value. This differs from a percentage value in the way it inherits: when a numerical value is specified, child elements will inherit the factor itself, not the resultant value (as is the case with percentage and other units).

Negative values are not allowed.

The three rules in the example below have the same resultant line height:

```
DIV { line-height: 1.2; font-size: 10pt }      /* number */
DIV { line-height: 1.2em; font-size: 10pt }    /* length */
DIV { line-height: 120%; font-size: 10pt }     /* percentage */
```

A value of 'normal' sets the 'line-height' to a reasonable value for the element's font. It is suggested that UAs set the 'normal' value to be a number in the range of 1.0 to 1.2.

See the section 4.4 for a description on how 'line-height' influences the formatting of a block-level element.

5.5 Box properties

The box properties set the size, circumference and position of the boxes that represent elements. See the formatting model (section 4) for examples on how to use the box properties.

The margin properties set the margin of an element. The 'margin' property sets the margin for all four sides while the other margin properties only set their respective side.

The padding properties describe how much space to insert between the border and the content (e.g., text or image). The 'padding' property sets the padding for all four sides while the other padding properties only set their respective side.

The border properties set the borders of an element. Each element has four borders, one on each side, that are defined by their width, color and style.

The 'width' and 'height' properties set the size of the box, and the 'float' and 'clear' properties can alter the position of elements.

5.5.1 'margin-top'

Value: <length> | <percentage> | auto
Initial: 0
Applies to: all elements
Inherited: no
Percentage values: refer to width of the closest block-level ancestor

This property sets the top margin of an element:

```
H1 { margin-top: 2em }
```

A negative value is allowed, but there may be implementation-specific limits.

5.5.2 'margin-right'

Value: <length> | <percentage> | auto
Initial: 0
Applies to: all elements
Inherited: no
Percentage values: refer to width of closest block-level ancestor

This property sets the right margin of an element:

```
H1 { margin-right: 12.3% }
```

A negative value is allowed, but there may be implementation-specific limits.

5.5.3 'margin-bottom'

Value: <length> | <percentage> | auto
Initial: 0
Applies to: all elements
Inherited: no
Percentage values: refer to width of closest block-level ancestor

This property sets the bottom margin of an element:

```
H1 { margin-bottom: 3px }
```

A negative value is allowed, but there may be implementation-specific limits.

5.5.4 'margin-left'

Value: <length> | <percentage> | auto
Initial: 0
Applies to: all elements
Inherited: no
Percentage values: refer to width of closest block-level ancestor

This property sets the left margin of an element:

```
H1 { margin-left: 2em }
```

A negative value is allowed, but there may be implementation-specific limits.

5.5.5 'margin'

Value: [<length> | <percentage> | auto]{1,4}
Initial: not defined for shorthand properties
Applies to: all elements
Inherited: no
Percentage values: refer to width of closest block-level ancestor

The 'margin' property is a shorthand property for setting 'margin-top', 'margin-right', 'margin-bottom' and 'margin-left' at the same place in the style sheet.

If four length values are specified they apply to top, right, bottom and left respectively. If there is only one value, it applies to all sides, if there are two or three, the missing values are taken from the opposite side.

```
BODY { margin: 2em } /* all margins set to 2em */
BODY { margin: 1em 2em } /* top & bottom = 1em, right & left = 2em */
BODY { margin: 1em 2em 3em } /* top=1em, right=2em, bottom=3em, left=2em */
```

The last rule of the example above is equivalent to the example below:

```
BODY {
  margin-top: 1em;
  margin-right: 2em;
  margin-bottom: 3em;
  margin-left: 2em;           /* copied from opposite side (right) */
}
```

Negative margin values are allowed, but there may be implementation-specific limits.

5.5.6 'padding-top'

Value: <length> | <percentage>
Initial: 0
Applies to: all elements
Inherited: no
Percentage values: refer to width of closest block-level ancestor

This property sets the top padding of an element.

```
BLOCKQUOTE { padding-top: 0.3em }
```

Padding values cannot be negative.

5.5.7 'padding-right'

Value: <length> | <percentage>
Initial: 0
Applies to: all elements
Inherited: no
Percentage values: refer to width of closest block-level ancestor

This property sets the right padding of an element.

```
BLOCKQUOTE { padding-right: 10px }
```

Padding values cannot be negative.

5.5.8 'padding-bottom'

Value: <length> | <percentage>
Initial: 0
Applies to: all elements
Inherited: no
Percentage values: refer to width of closest block-level ancestor

This property sets the bottom padding of an element.

```
BLOCKQUOTE { padding-bottom: 2em }
```

Padding values cannot be negative.

5.5.9 'padding-left'

Value: <length> | <percentage>
Initial: 0
Applies to: all elements
Inherited: no
Percentage values: refer to width of closest block-level ancestor

This property sets the left padding of an element.

```
BLOCKQUOTE { padding-left: 20% }
```

Padding values cannot be negative.

5.5.10 'padding'

Value: [<length> | <percentage>]{1,4}
Initial: not defined for shorthand properties
Applies to: all elements
Inherited: no
Percentage values: refer to width of closest block-level ancestor

The 'padding' property is a shorthand property for setting 'padding-top', 'padding-right', 'padding-bottom' and 'padding-left' at the same place in the style sheet.

If four values are specified they apply to top, right, bottom and left respectively. If there is only one value, it applies to all sides, if there are two or three, the missing values are taken from the opposite side.

The surface of the padding area is set with the 'background' property:

```
H1 {
    background: white;
    padding: 1em 2em;
}
```

The example above sets a '1em' padding vertically ('padding-top' and 'padding-bottom') and a '2em' padding horizontally ('padding-right' and 'padding-left'). The 'em' unit is relative to the element's font size: '1em' is equal to the size of the font in use.

Padding values cannot be negative.

5.5.11 'border-top-width'

Value: thin | medium | thick | <length>
Initial: 'medium'
Applies to: all elements
Inherited: no
Percentage values: N/A

This property sets the width of an element's top border. The width of the keyword values are UA dependent, but the following holds: 'thin' <= 'medium' <= 'thick'.

The keyword widths are constant throughout a document:

```
H1 { border: solid thick red }
P  { border: solid thick blue }
```

In the example above, 'H1' and 'P' elements will have the same border width regardless of font size. To achieve relative widths, the 'em' unit can be used:

```
H1 { border: solid 0.5em }
```

Border widths cannot be negative.

5.5.12 'border-right-width'

Value: thin | medium | thick | <length>
Initial: 'medium'
Applies to: all elements
Inherited: no
Percentage values: N/A

This property sets the width of an element's right border. Otherwise it is equivalent to the 'border-top-width'.

5.5.13 'border-bottom-width'

Value: thin | medium | thick | <length>
Initial: 'medium'
Applies to: all elements
Inherited: no
Percentage values: N/A

This property sets the width of an element's bottom border. Otherwise it is equivalent to the 'border-top-width'.

5.5.14 'border-left-width'

Value: thin | medium | thick | <length>
Initial: 'medium'
Applies to: all elements
Inherited: no
Percentage values: N/A

This property sets the width of an element's left border. Otherwise it is equivalent to the 'border-top-width'.

5.5.15 'border-width'

Value: [thin | medium | thick | <length>]{1,4}
Initial: not defined for shorthand properties
Applies to: all elements
Inherited: no
Percentage values: N/A

This property is a shorthand property for setting 'border-width-top', 'border-width-right', 'border-width-bottom' and 'border-width-left' at the same place in the style sheet.

There can be from one to four values, with the following interpretation:

• one value: all four border widths are set to that value

- two values: top and bottom border widths are set to the first value, right and left are set to the second

- three values: top is set to the first, right and left are set to the second, bottom is set to the third

- four values: top, right, bottom and left, respectively

In the examples below, the comments indicate the resulting widths of the top, right, bottom and left borders:

```
H1 { border-width: thin }                 /* thin thin thin thin */
H1 { border-width: thin thick }           /* thin thick thin thick */
H1 { border-width: thin thick medium }    /* thin thick medium thin */
H1 { border-width: thin thick medium thin } /* thin thick medium thin */
```

Border widths cannot be negative.

5.5.16 'border-color'

Value: <color>{1,4}
Initial: the value of the 'color' property
Applies to: all elements
Inherited: no
Percentage values: N/A

The 'border-color' property sets the color of the four borders. 'border-color' can have from one to four values, and the values are set on the different sides as for 'border-width' above.

If no color value is specified, the value of the 'color' property of the element itself will take its place:

```
P {
   color: black;
   background: white;
   border: solid;
}
```

In the above example, the border will be a solid black line.

5.5.17 'border-style'

Value: none | dotted | dashed | solid | double | groove | ridge | inset | outset
Initial: none

Applies to: all elements
Inherited: no
Percentage values: N/A

The 'border-style' property sets the style of the four borders. It can have from one to four values, and the values are set on the different sides as for 'border-width' above.

```
#xy34 { border-style: solid dotted }
```

In the above example, the horizontal borders will be 'solid' and the vertical borders will be 'dotted'.

Since the initial value of the border styles is 'none', no borders will be visible unless the border style is set.

The border styles mean:

  no border is drawn (regardless of the 'border-width' value)

dotted

  the border is a dotted line drawn on top of the background of the element

dashed

  the border is a dashed line drawn on top of the background of the element

solid

  the border is a solid line

double

  the border is a double line drawn on top of the background of the element. The sum of the two single lines and the space between equals the <border-width> value.

groove

  a 3D groove is drawn in colors based on the <color> value.

ridge

  a 3D ridge is drawn in colors based on the <color> value.

inset

  a 3D inset is drawn in colors based on the <color> value.

outset

> a 3D outset is drawn in colors based on the <color> value.

CSS1 core: UAs may interpret all of 'dotted', 'dashed', 'double', 'groove', 'ridge', 'inset' and 'outset' as 'solid'.

5.5.18 'border-top'

Value: <border-top-width> || <border-style> || <color>
Initial: not defined for shorthand properties
Applies to: all elements
Inherited: no
Percentage values: N/A

This is a shorthand property for setting the width, style and color of an element's top border.

```
H1 { border-bottom: thick solid red }
```

The above rule will set the width, style and color of the border below the H1 element. Omitted values will be set to their initial values:

```
H1 { border-bottom: thick solid }
```

Since the color value is omitted in the example above, the border color will be the same as the 'color' value of the element itself.

Note that while the 'border-style' property accepts up to four values, this property only accepts one style value.

5.5.19 'border-right'

Value: <border-right-width> || <border-style> || <color>
Initial: not defined for shorthand properties
Applies to: all elements
Inherited: no
Percentage values: N/A

This is a shorthand property for setting the width, style and color of an element's right border. Otherwise it is equivalent to the 'border-top'.

5.5.20 'border-bottom'

Value: <border-bottom-width> || <border-style> || <color>
Initial: not defined for shorthand properties
Applies to: all elements
Inherited: no
Percentage values: N/A

This is a shorthand property for setting the width, style and color of an element's bottom border. Otherwise it is equivalent to the 'border-top'.

5.5.21 'border-left'

Value: <border-left-width> || <border-style> || <color>
Initial: not defined for shorthand properties
Applies to: all elements
Inherited: no
Percentage values: N/A

This is a shorthand property for setting the width, style and color of an element's left border. Otherwise it is equivalent to the 'border-top'.

5.5.22 'border'

Value: <border-width> || <border-style> || <color>
Initial: not defined for shorthand properties
Applies to: all elements
Inherited: no
Percentage values: N/A

The 'border' property is a shorthand property for setting the same width, color and style on all four borders of an element. For example, the first rule below is equivalent to the set of four rules shown after it:

```
P { border: solid red }
P {
  border-top: solid red;
  border-right: solid red;
  border-bottom: solid red;
  border-left: solid red
```

}

Unlike the shorthand 'margin' and 'padding' properties, the 'border' property cannot set different values on the four borders. To do so, one or more of the other border properties must be used.

Since the properties to some extent have overlapping functionality, the order in which the rules are specified becomes important. Consider this example:

```
BLOCKQUOTE {
    border-color: red;
    border-left: double
    color: black;
}
```

In the above example, the color of the left border will be black, while the other borders are red. This is due to 'border-left' setting the width, style and color. Since the color value is not specified on the 'border-left' property, it will be taken from the 'color' property. The fact that the 'color' property is set after the 'border-left' property is not relevant.

Note that while the 'border-width' property accepts up to four length values, this property only accepts one.

5.5.23 'width'

Value: <length> | <percentage> | auto
Initial: auto
Applies to: block-level and replaced elements
Inherited: no
Percentage values: refer to parent element's width

This property can be applied to text elements, but it is most useful with replaced elements such as images. The width is to be enforced by scaling the image if necessary. When scaling, the aspect ratio of the image is preserved if the 'height' property is 'auto'.

Example:

```
IMG.icon { width: 100px }
```

If the 'width' and 'height' of a replaced element are both 'auto', these properties will be set to the intrinsic dimensions of the element.

Negative values are not allowed.

See the formatting model (section 4) for a description of the relationship between this property and the margin and padding.

5.5.24 'height'

Value: <length> | auto
Initial: auto
Applies to: block-level and replaced elements
Inherited: no
Percentage values: N/A

This property can be applied to text, but it is most useful with replaced elements such as images. The height is to be enforced by scaling the image if necessary. When scaling, the aspect ratio of the image is preserved if the 'width' property is 'auto'.

Example:

```
IMG.icon { height: 100px }
```

If the 'width' and 'height' of a replaced element are both 'auto', these properties will be set to the intrinsic dimensions of the element.

If applied to a textual element, the height can be enforced with e.g. a scrollbar.

Negative values are not allowed.

CSS1 core: UAs may ignore the 'height' property (i.e., treat it as 'auto') if the element is not a replaced element.

5.5.25 'float'

Value: left | right | none
Initial: none
Applies to: all elements
Inherited: no
Percentage values: N/A

With the value 'none', the element will be displayed where it appears in the text. With a value of 'left' ('right') the element will be moved to the left (right) and the text will wrap on the right (left) side of the element. With a value of 'left' or 'right', the element is treated as block-level (i.e. the 'display' property is ignored). See section 4.1.4 for a full specification.

```
IMG.icon {
```

```
    float: left;
    margin-left: 0;
}
```

The above example will place all IMG elements with 'CLASS=icon' along the left side of the parent element.

This property is most often used with inline images, but also applies to text elements.

5.5.26 'clear'

Value: none | left | right | both
Initial: none
Applies to: all elements
Inherited: no
Percentage values: N/A

This property specifies if an element allows floating elements on its sides. More specifically, the value of this property lists the sides where floating elements are not accepted. With 'clear' set to 'left', an element will be moved below any floating element on the left side. With 'clear' set to 'none', floating elements are allowed on all sides. Example:

```
    H1 { clear: left }
```

5.6 Classification properties

These properties classify elements into categories more than they set specific visual parameters.

The list-style properties describe how list items (i.e. elements with a 'display' value of 'list-item') are formatted. The list-style properties can be set on any element, and it will inherit normally down the tree. However, they will only be have effect on elements with a 'display' value of 'list-item'. In HTML this is typically the case for the 'LI' element.

5.6.1 'display'

Value: block | inline | list-item | none
Initial: block
Applies to: all elements

Inherited: no
Percentage values: N/A

This property describes how/if an element is displayed on the canvas (which may be on a printed page, a computer display etc.).

An element with a 'display' value of 'block' opens a new box. The box is positioned relative to adjacent boxes according to the CSS formatting model. Typically, elements like 'H1' and 'P' are of type 'block'. A value of 'list-item' is similar to 'block' except that a list-item marker is added. In HTML, 'LI' will typically have this value.

An element with a 'display' value of 'inline' results in a new inline box on the same line as the previous content. The box is dimensioned according to the formatted size of the content. If the content is text, it may span several lines, and there will be a box on each line. The margin, border and padding properties apply to 'inline' elements, but will not have any effect at the line breaks.

A value of 'none' turns off the display of the element, including children elements and the surrounding box.

```
P   { display: block }
EM  { display: inline }
LI  { display: list-item }
IMG { display: none }
```

The last rule turns off the display of images.

The initial value of 'display' is 'block', but a UA will typically have default values for all HTML elements according to the suggested rendering of elements in the HTML specification [2].

CSS1 core: UAs may ignore 'display' and use only the UA's default values. (See section 7.)

5.6.2 'white-space'

Value: normal | pre | nowrap
Initial: normal
Applies to: block-level elements
Inherited: yes
Percentage values: N/A

This property declares how whitespace inside the element is handled: the 'normal' way (where whitespace is collapsed), as 'pre' (which behaves like the 'PRE' element in HTML) or as 'nowrap' (where wrapping is done only through BR elements):

```
PRE { white-space: pre }
```

```
P    { white-space: normal }
```

The initial value of 'white-space' is 'normal', but a UA will typically have default values for all HTML elements according to the suggested rendering of elements in the HTML specification [2].

CSS1 core: UAs may ignore the 'white-space' property in author's and reader's style sheets, and use the UA's default values instead. (See section 7.)

5.6.3 'list-style-type'

Value: disc | circle | square | decimal | lower-roman | upper-roman | lower-alpha | upper-alpha | none
Initial: disc
Applies to: elements with 'display' value 'list-item'
Inherited: yes
Percentage values: N/A

This property is used to determine the appearance of the list-item marker if 'list-style-image' is 'none' or if the image pointed to by the URL cannot be displayed.

```
OL { list-style-type: decimal }      /* 1 2 3 4 5 etc. */
OL { list-style-type: lower-alpha }  /* a b c d e etc. */
OL { list-style-type: lower-roman }  /* i ii iii iv v etc. */
```

5.6.4 'list-style-image'

Value: <url> | none
Initial: none
Applies to: elements with 'display' value 'list-item'
Inherited: yes
Percentage values: N/A

This property sets the image that will be used as the list-item marker. When the image is available it will replace the marker set with the 'list-style-type' marker.

```
UL { list-style-image: url(http://png.com/ellipse.png) }
```

5.6.5 'list-style-position'

Value: inside | outside
Initial: outside
Applies to: elements with 'display' value 'list-item'
Inherited: yes
Percentage values: N/A

The value of 'list-style-position' determines how the list-item marker is drawn with regard to the content. For a formatting example see section 4.1.3.

5.6.6 'list-style'

Value: [disc | circle | square | decimal | lower-roman | upper-roman | lower-alpha | upper-alpha | none] || [inside | outside] || [<url> | none]
Initial: not defined for shorthand properties
Applies to: elements with 'display' value 'list-item'
Inherited: yes
Percentage values: N/A

The 'list-style' property is a shorthand notation for setting the three properties 'list-style-type', 'list-style-image' and 'list-style-position' at the same place in the style sheet.

```
UL { list-style: upper-roman inside }
UL UL { list-style: circle outside }
LI.square { list-style: square }
```

Setting 'list-style' directly on 'LI' elements can have unexpected results. Consider:

```
<STYLE TYPE="text/css">
  OL.alpha LI   { list-style: lower-alpha }
  UL LI         { list-style: disc }
</STYLE>
<BODY>
  <OL CLASS=alpha>
    <LI>level 1
    <UL>
        <LI>level 2
    </UL>
  </OL>
</BODY>
```

Since the specificity (as defined in the cascading order) is higher for the first rule in the style sheet in the example above, it will override the second rule on all 'LI' elements and only 'lower-alpha' list styles will be used. It is therefore recommended to set 'list-style' only on the list type elements:

```
OL.alpha   { list-style: lower-alpha }
UL         { list-style: disc }
```

In the above example, inheritance will transfer the 'list-style' values from 'OL' and 'UL' elements to 'LI' elements.

A URL value can be combined with any other value:

```
UL { list-style: url(http://png.com/ellipse.png) disc }
```

In the example above, the 'disc' will be used when the image is unavailable.

Chapter 6

Units

6.1 Length units

The format of a length value is an optional sign character ('+' or '-', with '+' being the default) immediately followed by a number (with or without a decimal point) immediately followed by a unit identifier (a two-letter abbreviation). After a '0' number, the unit identifier is optional.

Some properties allow negative length units, but this may complicate the formatting model and there may be implementation-specific limits. If a negative length value cannot be supported, it should be clipped to the nearest value that can be supported.

There are two types of length units: relative and absolute. Relative units specify a length relative to another length property. Style sheets that use relative units will more easily scale from one medium to another (e.g. from a computer display to a laser printer). Percentage units (described below) and keyword values (e.g. 'x-large') offer similar advantages.

These relative units are supported:

```
H1 { margin: 0.5em }      /* ems, the height of the element's font */
H1 { margin: 1ex }        /* x-height, ~ the height of the letter 'x' */
P  { font-size: 12px }    /* pixels, relative to canvas */
```

The relative units 'em' and 'ex' are relative to the font size of the element itself. The only exception to this rule in CSS1 is the 'font-size' property where 'em' and 'ex' values refer to the font size of the parent element.

Pixel units, as used in the last rule, are relative to the resolution of the canvas, i.e. most often a computer display. If the pixel density of the output device is very different from that of a typical computer display, the UA should rescale pixel values. The suggested reference pixel is the visual angle of one pixel on a device with a pixel density of 90dpi and a distance from the reader of an arm's length. For a nominal arm's length of 28 inches, the visual angle is about 0.0227 degrees.

Child elements inherit the computed value, not the relative value:

```
BODY {
   font-size: 12pt;
   text-indent: 3em;    /* i.e. 36pt */
}
H1 { font-size: 15pt }
```

In the example above, the 'text-indent' value of 'H1' elements will be 36pt, not 45pt.

Absolute length units are only useful when the physical properties of the output medium are known. These absolute units are supported:

```
H1 { margin: 0.5in }       /* inches, 1in = 2.54cm */
H2 { line-height: 3cm }    /* centimeters */
H3 { word-spacing: 4mm }   /* millimeters */
H4 { font-size: 12pt }     /* points, 1pt = 1/72 in */
H4 { font-size: 1pc }      /* picas, 1pc = 12pt */
```

In cases where the specified length cannot be supported, UAs should try to approximate. For all CSS1 properties, further computations and inheritance should be based on the approximated value.

6.2 Percentage units

The format of a percentage value is an optional sign character ('+' or '-', with '+' being the default) immediately followed by a number (with or without a decimal point) immediately followed by '%'.

Percentage values are always relative to another value, for example a length unit. Each property that allows percentage units also defines what value the percentage value refer to. Most often this is the font size of the element itself:

```
P { line-height: 120% }    /* 120% of the element's 'font-size' */
```

In all inherited CSS1 properties, if the value is specified as a percentage, child elements inherit the resultant value, not the percentage value.

6.3 Color units

A color is a either a keyword or a numerical RGB specification.

The suggested list of keyword color names is: aqua, black, blue, fuchsia, gray, green, lime, maroon, navy, olive, purple, red, silver, teal, white, and yellow. These 16 colors are taken from the Windows VGA palette, and their RGB values are not defined in this specification.

```
BODY {color: black; background: white }
H1 { color: maroon }
H2 { color: olive }
```

The RGB color model is being used in numerical color specifications. These examples all specify the same color:

```
EM { color: #f00 }              /* #rgb */
EM { color: #ff0000 }           /* #rrggbb */
EM { color: rgb(255,0,0) }      /* integer range 0-255 */
EM { color: rgb(100%, 0%, 0%) } /* float range 0.0%-100.0% */
```

The format of an RGB value in hexadecimal notation is a '#' immediately followed by either three or six hexadecimal characters. The three-digit RGB notation (#rgb) is converted into six-digit form (#rrggbb) by replicating digits, not by adding zeros. For example, #fb0 expands to #ffbb00. This makes sure that white (#ffffff) can be specified with the short notation (#fff) and removes any dependencies on the color depth of the display.

The format of an RGB value in the functional notation is 'rgb(' followed by a comma-separated list of three numerical values (either three integer values in the range of 0-255, or three percentage values in the range of 0.0% to 100.0%) followed by ')'. Whitespace characters are allowed around the numerical values.

Values outside the numerical ranges should be clipped. The three rules below are therefore equivalent:

```
EM { color: rgb(255,0,0) }      /* integer range 0-255 */
EM { color: rgb(300,0,0) }      /* clipped to 255 */
EM { color: rgb(110%, 0%, 0%) } /* clipped to 100% */
```

RGB colors are specified in the sRGB color space [9]. UAs may vary in the fidelity with which they represent these colors, but use of sRGB provides an unambiguous and objectively measurable definition of what the color should be, which can be related to international standards [10].

UAs may limit their efforts in displaying colors to performing a gamma-correction on them. sRGB specifies a display gamma of 2.2 under specified viewing conditions. UAs adjust the colors given in CSS such that, in combination with an output device's "natural" display gamma, an effective display gamma of 2.2 is produced. Appendix D gives further details of this. Note that only colors specified in CSS are affected; e.g., images are expected to carry their own color information.

6.4 URL

A Uniform Resource Locator (URL) is identified with a functional notation:

```
BODY { background: url(http://www.bg.com/pinkish.gif) }
```

The format of a URL value is 'url(' followed by optional white space followed by an optional single quote (') or double quote (") character followed by the URL itself (as defined in [11]) followed by an optional single quote (') or double quote (") character followed by optional whitespace followed by ')'. Quote characters that are not part of the URL itself must be balanced.

Parentheses, commas, whitespace characters, single quotes (') and double quotes (") appearing in a URL must be escaped with a backslash: '\(', '\)', '\,'.

Partial URLs are interpreted relative to the source of the style sheet, not relative to the document:

```
BODY { background: url(yellow) }
```

Chapter 7

CSS1 Conformance

A User Agent that uses CSS1 to display documents conforms to the CSS1 specification if it:

- attempts to fetch all referenced style sheets and parse them according to this specification

- sorts the declarations according to the cascading order

- implements the CSS1 functionality within the constraints of the presentation medium (see explanation below).

A User Agent that outputs CSS1 style sheets conforms to the CSS1 specification if it:

- outputs valid CSS1 style sheets

A User Agent that uses CSS1 to display documents *and* outputs CSS1 style sheets conforms to the CSS1 specification if it meets both sets of conformance requirements.

A UA does not have to implement all the functionality of CSS1: it can conform to CSS1 by implementing the core functionality. The core functionality consists of the whole CSS1 specification except those parts explicitly excluded. In the text, those parts are marked with *"CSS1 core:"* followed by an explanation of what functionality is outside the core functionality. The set of features excluded from the core functionality is called CSS1 advanced features.

This section only defines conformance to CSS1. There will be other levels of CSS in the future that may require a UA to implement a different set of features in order to conform.

Examples of constraints of the presentation medium are: limited resources (fonts, color) and limited resolution (so margins may not be accurate). In these cases, the UA should approximate the style sheet values. Also, different user interface paradigms may have their own constraints: a VR browser may rescale the document based on its "distance" from the user.

UAs may offer readers additional choices on presentation. For example, the UA may provide options for readers with visual impairments or may provide the choice to disable blinking.

Note that CSS1 does not specify all aspects of formatting. E.g., the UA is free to select a letter-spacing algorithm.

This specification also recommends, but doesn't require, that a UA:

- allows the reader to specify personal style sheets

- allows individual style sheets to be turned on and off

The above conformance rules describe only functionality, not user interface.

7.1 Forward-compatible parsing

This specification defines CSS level 1. It is expected that higher levels of CSS, with additional features, will be defined in the future. To ensure that UAs supporting just CSS1 will be able to read style sheets containing higher level features, this section defines what the UA does when it encounters certain constructs that are not valid in CSS level 1.

- a declaration with an unknown property is ignored. For example, if the style sheet is

```
H1 { color: red; rotation: 70deg }
```

the UA will treat this as if the style sheet had been

```
H1 { color: red; }
```

- illegal values, *or values with illegal parts*, are treated as if the declaration weren't there at all:

```
IMG { float: left }        /* CSS1 */
IMG { float: left top }    /* "top" is not a value of 'float' */
IMG { background: "red" }  /* keywords cannot be quoted in CSS1 */
IMG { border-width: 3 }    /* a unit must be specified for length values */
```

In the above example, a CSS1 parser would honor the first rule and ignore the rest, as if the style sheet had been

```
IMG { float: left }
IMG { }
IMG { }
IMG { }
```

A UA conforming to a future CSS specification may accept one or more of the other rules as well.

- an invalid at-keyword is ignored together with everything following it, up to and including the next semicolon (;) or brace pair ({...}), whichever comes first. For example, assume the style sheet reads:

```
@three-dee {
  @background-lighting {
    azimuth: 30deg;
    elevation: 190deg;
  }
  H1 { color: red }
}
H1 {color: blue}
```

The '@three-dee' is illegal according to CSS1. Therefore, the whole at-rule (up to, and including, the third right curly brace) is ignored. The CSS1 UA skips it, effectively reducing the style sheet to:

```
H1 {color: blue}
```

In more detail:

A CSS style sheet, for any version of CSS, consists of a list of *statements*. There are two kinds of statements: *at-rules* and *rulesets*. There may be whitespace (spaces, tabs, newlines) around the statements.

CSS style sheets are often embedded in HTML documents, and to be able to hide style sheets from older UAs, it is convenient put the style sheets inside HTML comments. The HTML comment tokens "<!—" and "—>" may occur before, after, and in between the statements. They may have whitespace around them.

At-rules start with an *at-keyword*, which is an identifier with an '@' at the start (for example: '@import', '@page'). An identifier consists of letters, digits, dashes and escaped characters (defined below).

An at-rule consists of everything up to and including the next semicolon (;) or the next block (defined shortly), whichever comes first. A CSS1 UA that encounters an at-rule that starts with an at-keyword other than '@import' ignores the whole of the at-rule and continue parsing after it. It also ignores any at-rule that starts with '@import' if it doesn't occur at the top of the style sheet, i.e., if it occurs after any rules (even ignored rules). Here is an example.

Assume a CSS1 parser encounters this style sheet:

```
@import "subs.css";
H1 { color: blue }
@import "list.css";
```

The second '@import' is illegal according to CSS1. The CSS1 parser skips the whole at-rule, effectively reducing the style sheet to:

```
@import "subs.css";
H1 {color: blue}
```

A *block* starts with a left curly brace ({) and ends with the matching right curly brace (}). In between there may be any characters, except that parentheses (()), brackets ([]) and braces ({}) always occur in matching pairs and may be nested. Single (') and double quotes (") also occur in matching pairs, and characters between them are parsed as a *string* (see the tokenizer in appendix B for a definition of string). Here is an example of a block; note that the right brace between the quotes does not match the opening brace of the block, and that the second single quote is an escaped character, and thus doesn't match the opening quote:

```
{ causta: "}" + ({7} * '\")  }
```

A ruleset consists of a *selector-string* followed by a *declaration-block*. The selector-string consists of everything up to (but not including) the first left curly brace ({). A ruleset that starts with a selector-string that is not valid CSS1 is skipped.

For example, assume a CSS1 parser encounters this style sheet:

```
H1 { color: blue }
P[align], UL { color: red; font-size: large }
P EM { font-weight: bold }
```

The second line contains a selector-string that is illegal in CSS1. The CSS1 UA will skip the ruleset, reducing the style sheet to:

```
H1 { color: blue }
P EM { font-weight: bold }
```

A declaration-block starts with a left curly brace ({) and ends with the matching right curly brace (}). In between there is a list of zero or more *declarations*, separated by semicolons (;).

A declaration consists of a *property*, a colon (:) and a *value*. Around each of these there may be whitespace. A property is an identifier, as defined earlier. Any character may occur in the value, but parentheses (()), brackets ([]), braces ({}), single quotes (') and double quotes (") must come in matching pairs. Parentheses, brackets, and braces may be nested. Inside the quotes, characters are parsed as a string.

To ensure that new properties and new values for existing properties can be added in the future, a UA must skip a declaration with an invalid property name or an invalid value. Every CSS1 property has its own syntactic and semantic restrictions on the values it accepts.

For example, assume a CSS1 parser encounters this style sheet:

```
H1 { color: red; font-style: 12pt }
P { color: blue;   font-vendor: any;   font-variant: small-caps }
EM EM { font-style: normal }
```

The second declaration on the first line has an invalid value '12pt'. The second declaration on the second line contains an undefined property 'font-vendor'. The CSS1 parser will skip these declarations, reducing the style sheet to:

```
H1 { color: red; }
P { color: blue;   font-variant: small-caps }
EM EM { font-style: normal }
```

Comments (see section 1.7) can occur anywhere where whitespace can occur and are considered to be whitespace. CSS1 defines additional places where whitespace can occur (such as inside values) and comments are allowed there as well.

The following rules always hold:

- All CSS style sheets are case-insensitive, except for parts that are not under the control of CSS. I.e., in CSS1, font family names and URLs can be case-sensitive. Also, the case-sensitivity of the CLASS and ID attributes is under the control of HTML [2].

- in CSS1, selectors (element names, classes and IDs) can contain only the characters A-Z, 0-9, and Unicode characters 161-255, plus dash (-); they cannot start with a dash or a digit; they can also contain escaped characters and any Unicode character as a numeric code (see next item).

- the backslash followed by at most four hexadecimal digits (0..9A..F) stands for the Unicode character with that number.

- any character except a hexadecimal digit can be escaped to remove its special meaning, by putting a backslash in front, Example: "\"" is a string consisting of one double quote.

- the two preceding items define *backslash-escapes*. Backslash-escapes are always considered to be part of an identifier, except inside strings (i.e., "\7B" is not punctuation, even though "{" is, and "\32" is allowed at the start of a class name, even though "2" is not).

Note: The CLASS attribute of HTML allows more characters in a class name than the set allowed for selectors above. In CSS1, these characters have to be escaped or written as Unicode numbers: "B&W?" can be written as "B\&W\?" or "B\26W\3F", "??????" (Greek: "kouros") has to be written as "\3BA\3BF\3C5\3C1\3BF\3C2". It is expected that in later versions of CSS more characters can be entered directly.

Appendix B gives a grammar for CSS1.

Chapter 8

References

[1] W3C resource page on web style sheets (http://www.w3.org/Style)

[2] "HTML 4.0 Specification", D. Raggett, A. Le Hors, I. Jacobs, December 1997. Available at http://www.w3.org/TR/REC-html40/.

[3] T Berners-Lee, D Connolly: "Hypertext Markup Language—2.0", RFC 1866, MIT/W3C, November 1995. The specification is also available in hypertext form (http://www.w3.org/MarkUp/html-spec/html-spec_toc.html)

[4] F Yergeau, G Nicol, G Adams, M Dürst: "Internationalization of the Hypertext Markup Language" (ftp://ds.internic.net/rfc/rfc2070.txt).

[5] ISO 8879:1986. Information Processing—Text and Office Systems—Standard Generalized Markup Language (SGML)

[6] ISO/IEC 10179:1996 Information technology—Processing languages—Document Style Semantics and Specification Language (DSSSL).

[7] ISO/IEC 9899:1990 Programming language—C.

[8] The Unicode Consortium, "The Unicode Standard—Worldwide Character Encoding—Version 1.0", Addison-Wesley, Volume 1, 1991, Volume 2, 1992.

[9] "A Standard Default color Space for the Internet", version 1.10, M. Stokes, M. Anderson, S. Chandrasekar, and R. Motta, 5 November 1996.

[10] CIE Publication 15.2–1986, "Colorimetry, Second Edition", ISBN 3-900-734-00-3 (http://www.hike.te.chiba-u.ac.jp/ikeda/CIE/publ/abst/15-2-86.html)

[11] T Berners-Lee, L Masinter, M McCahill: "Uniform Resource Locators (URL)", RFC 1738, CERN, Xerox Corporation, University of Minnesota, December 1994

[12] "PNG (Portable Network Graphics) Specification, Version 1.0 specification" (http://www.w3.org/TR/REC-png-multi.html)

[13] Charles A. Poynton: "Gamma correction on the Macintosh Platform" (ftp://ftp.inforamp.net/pub/users/poynton/doc/Mac/Mac_gamma.pdf)

[14] International Color Consortium: "ICC Profile Format Specification, version 3.2", 1995 (ftp://sgigate.sgi.com/pub/icc/ICC32.pdf)

[15] S C Johnson: "YACC—Yet another compiler compiler", Technical Report, Murray Hill, 1975

[16] "Flex: The Lexical Scanner Generator", Version 2.3.7, ISBN 1882114213

Chapter 9

Acknowledgments

During the short life of HTML, there have been several style sheet proposals to which this proposal is indebted. Especially the proposals from Robert Raisch, Joe English and Pei Wei were influential.

A number of people have contributed to the development of CSS1. We would especially like to thank: Terry Allen, Murray Altheim, Glenn Adams, Walter Bender, Tim Berners-Lee, Yves Bertot, Scott Bigham, Steve Byrne, Robert Cailliau, James Clark, Daniel Connolly, Donna Converse, Adam Costello, Todd Fahrner, Todd Freter, Roy Fielding, Neil Galarneau, Wayne Gramlich, Phill Hallam-Baker, Philipp Hoschka, Kevin Hughes, Scott Isaacs, Tony Jebson, William Johnston, Gilles Kahn, Philippe Kaplan, Phil Karlton, Evan Kirshenbaum, Yves Lafon, Murray Maloney, Lou Montulli, Colas Nahaboo, Henrik Frystyk Nielsen, David Perrell, William Perry, Scott Preece, Paul Prescod, Liam Quin, Vincent Quint, Jenny Raggett, Thomas Reardon, Cécile Roisin, Michael Seaton, David Seibert, David Siegel, David Singer, Benjamin Sittler, Jon Smirl, Charles Peyton Taylor, Irène Vatton, Daniel Veillard, Mandira Virmani, Greg Watkins, Mike Wexler, Lydja Williams, Brian Wilson, Chris Wilson, Lauren Wood and Stephen Zilles.

Three people deserve special mentioning: Dave Raggett (for his encouragement and work on HTML3), Chris Lilley (for his continued contributions, especially in the area of colors and fonts) and Steven Pemberton (for his organizational as well as creative skills).

Appendix A:
Sample Style Sheet for HTML 2.0

(This appendix is informative, not normative)

The following style sheet is written according to the suggested rendering in the HTML 2.0 [3] specification. Some styles, e.g. colors, have been added for completeness. It is suggested that a style sheet similar to the one below is used as the UA default.

```
BODY {
   margin: 1em;
   font-family: serif;
   line-height: 1.1;
   background: white;
   color: black;
}

H1, H2, H3, H4, H5, H6, P, UL, OL, DIR, MENU, DIV,
DT, DD, ADDRESS, BLOCKQUOTE, PRE, BR, HR, FORM, DL {
   display: block }

B, STRONG, I, EM, CITE, VAR, TT, CODE, KBD, SAMP,
IMG, SPAN { display: inline }

LI { display: list-item }

H1, H2, H3, H4 { margin-top: 1em; margin-bottom: 1em }
H5, H6 { margin-top: 1em }
H1 { text-align: center }
H1, H2, H4, H6 { font-weight: bold }
H3, H5 { font-style: italic }

H1 { font-size: xx-large }
H2 { font-size: x-large }
H3 { font-size: large }

B, STRONG { font-weight: bolder }   /* relative to the parent */
```

```
I, CITE, EM, VAR, ADDRESS, BLOCKQUOTE { font-style: italic }
PRE, TT, CODE, KBD, SAMP { font-family: monospace }

PRE { white-space: pre }

ADDRESS { margin-left: 3em }
BLOCKQUOTE { margin-left: 3em; margin-right: 3em }

UL, DIR { list-style: disc }
OL { list-style: decimal }
MENU { margin: 0 }              /* tight formatting */
LI { margin-left: 3em }

DT { margin-bottom: 0 }
DD { margin-top: 0; margin-left: 3em }

HR { border-top: solid }    /* 'border-bottom' could also have been used */

A:link { color: blue }           /* unvisited link */
A:visited { color: red }         /* visited links */
A:active { color: lime }         /* active links */

/* setting the anchor border around IMG elements
   requires contextual selectors */

A:link IMG { border: 2px solid blue }
A:visited IMG { border: 2px solid red }
A:active IMG { border: 2px solid lime }
```

Appendix B: CSS1 Grammar

(This appendix is normative)

The minimal CSS (i.e., any version of CSS) grammar that all implementations need to support is defined in section 7. The grammar below defines a much smaller language, a language that defines the syntax of CSS1.

It is in some sense, however, still a superset of CSS1: there are additional semantic constraints not expressed in this grammar. A conforming UA must also adhere to the forward-compatible parsing rules (section 7.1), the property and value notation (section 5) and the unit notation (section 6). In addition, HTML imposes restrictions, e.g., on the possible values of the CLASS attribute.

The grammar below is LL(1) (but note that most UA's should not use it directly, since it doesn't express the parsing conventions, only the CSS1 syntax). The format of the productions is optimized for human consumption and some shorthand notation beyond yacc [15] is used:

```
*   : 0 or more
+   : 1 or more
?   : 0 or 1
|   : separates alternatives
[]  : grouping
```

The productions are:

```
stylesheet
  : [CDO|CDC]* [ import [CDO|CDC]* ]* [ ruleset [CDO|CDC]* ]*
  ;
import
  : IMPORT_SYM [STRING|URL] ';'           /* E.g., @import url(fun.css); */
  ;
unary_operator
  : '-' | '+'
  ;
operator
  : '/' | ',' | /* empty */
```

```
  ;
property
  : IDENT
  ;
ruleset
  : selector [ ',' selector ]*
    '{' declaration [ ';' declaration ]* '}'
  ;
selector
  : simple_selector+ [ pseudo_element | solitary_pseudo_element ]?
  | solitary_pseudo_element
  ;
    /* An "id" is an ID that is attached to an element type
    ** on its left, as in: P#p007
    ** A "solitary_id" is an ID that is not so attached,
    ** as in: #p007
    ** Analogously for classes and pseudo-classes.
    */
simple_selector
  : element_name id? class? pseudo_class?     /* eg: H1.subject */
  | solitary_id class? pseudo_class?          /* eg: #xyz33 */
  | solitary_class pseudo_class?                    /* eg: .author */
  | solitary_pseudo_class              /* eg: :link */
  ;
element_name
  : IDENT
  ;
pseudo_class                               /* as in:  A:link */
  : LINK_PSCLASS_AFTER_IDENT
  | VISITED_PSCLASS_AFTER_IDENT
  | ACTIVE_PSCLASS_AFTER_IDENT
  ;
solitary_pseudo_class                      /* as in:  :link */
  : LINK_PSCLASS
  | VISITED_PSCLASS
  | ACTIVE_PSCLASS
  ;
```

```
class                                  /* as in:  P.note */
 : CLASS_AFTER_IDENT
 ;
solitary_class                         /* as in:  .note */
 : CLASS
 ;
pseudo_element                         /* as in:  P:first-line */
 : FIRST_LETTER_AFTER_IDENT
 | FIRST_LINE_AFTER_IDENT
 ;
solitary_pseudo_element                /* as in:  :first-line */
 : FIRST_LETTER
 | FIRST_LINE
 ;
   /* There is a constraint on the id and solitary_id that the
   ** part after the "#" must be a valid HTML ID value;
   ** e.g., "#x77" is OK, but "#77" is not.
   */
id
 : HASH_AFTER_IDENT
 ;
solitary_id
 : HASH
 ;
declaration
 : property ':' expr prio?
 | /* empty */                        /* Prevents syntax errors... */
 ;
prio
 : IMPORTANT_SYM              /* !important */
 ;
expr
 : term [ operator term ]*
 ;
term
 : unary_operator?
```

```
    [ NUMBER | STRING | PERCENTAGE | LENGTH | EMS | EXS
    | IDENT | hexcolor | URL | RGB ]
  ;
    /* There is a constraint on the color that it must
    ** have either 3 or 6 hex-digits (i.e., [0-9a-fA-F])
    ** after the "#"; e.g., "#000" is OK, but "#abcd" is not.
    */
hexcolor
  : HASH | HASH_AFTER_IDENT
  ;
```

The following is the tokenizer, written in flex [16] notation. Note that this assumes an 8-bit implementation of flex. The tokenizer is case-insensitive (flex command line option -i).

```
unicode              \\[0-9a-f]{1,4}
latin1               [¡-ÿ]
escape               {unicode}|\\[ -~¡-ÿ]
stringchar           {escape}|{latin1}|[ !#$%&(-~]
nmstrt               [a-z]|{latin1}|{escape}
nmchar               [-a-z0-9]|{latin1}|{escape}
ident        {nmstrt}{nmchar}*
name         {nmchar}+
d            [0-9]
notnm        [^-a-z0-9\\]|{latin1}
w            [ \t\n]*
num          {d}+|{d}*\.{d}+
string               \"({stringchar}|\')*\"|\'({stringchar}|\")*\'

%x COMMENT
%s AFTER_IDENT

%%
"/*"                        {BEGIN(COMMENT);}
<COMMENT>"*/"               {BEGIN(0);}
<COMMENT>\n                 {/* ignore */}
<COMMENT>.                  {/* ignore */}
@import                     {BEGIN(0); return IMPORT_SYM;}
"!"{w}important             {BEGIN(0); return IMPORTANT_SYM;}
{ident}                     {BEGIN(AFTER_IDENT); return IDENT;}
```

```
{string}                              {BEGIN(0); return STRING;}

{num}                     {BEGIN(0); return NUMBER;}
{num}"%"                              {BEGIN(0); return PERCENTAGE;}
{num}pt/{notnm}                       {BEGIN(0); return LENGTH;}
{num}mm/{notnm}                       {BEGIN(0); return LENGTH;}
{num}cm/{notnm}                       {BEGIN(0); return LENGTH;}
{num}pc/{notnm}                       {BEGIN(0); return LENGTH;}
{num}in/{notnm}                       {BEGIN(0); return LENGTH;}
{num}px/{notnm}                       {BEGIN(0); return LENGTH;}
{num}em/{notnm}                       {BEGIN(0); return EMS;}
{num}ex/{notnm}                       {BEGIN(0); return EXS;}

<AFTER_IDENT>":"link          {return LINK_PSCLASS_AFTER_IDENT;}
<AFTER_IDENT>":"visited   {return VISITED_PSCLASS_AFTER_IDENT;}
<AFTER_IDENT>":"active    {return ACTIVE_PSCLASS_AFTER_IDENT;}
<AFTER_IDENT>":"first-line    {return FIRST_LINE_AFTER_IDENT;}
<AFTER_IDENT>":"first-letter    {return FIRST_LETTER_AFTER_IDENT;}
<AFTER_IDENT>"#"{name}          {return HASH_AFTER_IDENT;}
<AFTER_IDENT>"."{name}          {return CLASS_AFTER_IDENT;}

":"link                       {BEGIN(AFTER_IDENT); return LINK_PSCLASS;}
":"visited                    {BEGIN(AFTER_IDENT); return VISITED_PSCLASS;}
":"active                     {BEGIN(AFTER_IDENT); return ACTIVE_PSCLASS;}
":"first-line                 {BEGIN(AFTER_IDENT); return FIRST_LINE;}
":"first-letter               {BEGIN(AFTER_IDENT); return FIRST_LETTER;}
"#"{name}                     {BEGIN(AFTER_IDENT); return HASH;}
"."{name}                     {BEGIN(AFTER_IDENT); return CLASS;}

url\({w}{string}{w}\)                                    |
url\({w}([^ \n\'\")]|\\\ |\\\'|\\\"|\\\))+{w}\)    {BEGIN(0); return URL;}
rgb\({w}{num}%?{w}\,{w}{num}%?{w}\,{w}{num}%?{w}\)  {BEGIN(0); return RGB;}

[-/+{};,#:]                   {BEGIN(0); return *yytext;}
[ \t]+                        {BEGIN(0); /* ignore whitespace */}
\n                    {BEGIN(0); /* ignore whitespace */}
\<\!\-\-                      {BEGIN(0); return CDO;}
\-\-\>                        {BEGIN(0); return CDC;}
```

.

```
{fprintf(stderr, "%d: Illegal character (%d)\n",
lineno, *yytext);}
```

Appendix C: Encoding

(This appendix is informative, not normative)

HTML documents may contain any of the about 30,000 different characters defined by Unicode. Many documents only need a few hundred. Many fonts also only contain just a few hundred glyphs. In combination with section 5.2, this appendix explains how the characters in the document and the glyphs in a font are matched.

Character encoding

The content of an HTML document is a sequence of *characters* and markup. To send it "over the wire", it is encoded as a sequence of bytes, using one of several possible *encodings*. The HTML document has to be decoded to find the characters. For example, in Western Europe it is customary to use the byte 224 for an a-with-grave-accent (à), but in Hebrew, it is more common to use 224 for an Aleph. In Japanese, the meaning of a byte usually depends on the bytes that preceded it. In some encodings, one character is encoded as two (or more) bytes.

The UA knows how to decode the bytes by looking at the "charset" parameter in the HTTP header. Typical encodings (charset values) are "ASCII" (for English), "ISO-8859-1" (for Western Europe), "ISO-8859-8" (for Hebrew), "Shift-JIS" (for Japanese).

HTML [2][4], allows some 30,000 different characters, namely those defined by Unicode. Not many documents will use that many different characters, and choosing the right encoding will usually ensure that the document only needs one byte per character. Occasional characters outside the encoded range can still be entered as numerical character references: 'Π' will always mean the Greek uppercase Pi, no matter what encoding was used. Note that this entails that UAs have to be prepared for any Unicode character, even if they only handle a few encodings.

Font encoding

A font doesn't contain *characters*, it contains pictures of characters, known as *glyphs*. The glyphs, in the form of outlines or bitmaps, constitute a particular representation of a character. Either explicitly or implicitly, each font has a table associated with it, the *font encoding table*, that tells for each glyph what character it is a representation for. In Type 1 fonts, the table is referred to as an *encoding vector*.

In fact, many fonts contain several glyphs for the same character. Which of those glyphs should be used depends either on the rules of the language, or on the preference of the designer.

In Arabic, for example, all letters have four different shapes, depending on whether the letter is used at the start of a word, in the middle, at the end, or in isolation. It is the same character in all cases, and thus there is only one character in the HTML document, but when printed, it looks differently each time.

There are also fonts that leave it to the graphic designer to choose from among various alternative shapes provided. Unfortunately, CSS1 doesn't yet provide the means to select those alternatives. Currently, it is always the default shape that is chosen from such fonts.

Font sets

To deal with the problem that a single font may not be enough to display all the characters in a document, or even a single element, CSS1 allows the use of *font sets*.

A font set in CSS1 is a list of fonts, all of the same style and size, that are tried in sequence to see if they contain a glyph for a certain character. An element that contains English text mixed with mathematical symbols may need a font set of two fonts, one containing letters and digits, the other containing mathematical symbols. See section 5.2 for a detailed description of the selection mechanism for font sets.

Here is an example of a font set suitable for a text that is expected to contain text with Latin characters, Japanese characters, and mathematical symbols:

```
BODY { font-family: Baskerville, Mincho, Symbol, serif }
```

The characters available in the Baskerville font (a font with only Latin characters) will be taken from that font, Japanese will be taken from Mincho, and the mathematical symbols will come from Symbol. Any other characters will (hopefully) come from the generic font family 'serif'. The 'serif' font family will also be used if one or more of the other fonts is unavailable.

Appendix D: Gamma Correction

(This appendix is informative, not normative)

See the Gamma Tutorial in the PNG specification [12] if you aren't already familiar with gamma issues.

In the computation, UAs displaying on a CRT may assume an ideal CRT and ignore any effects on apparent gamma caused by dithering. That means the minimal handling they need to do on current platforms is:

PC using MS-Windows

Unix using X11

Mac using QuickDraw

  apply gamma 1.39 [13] (ColorSync-savvy applications may simply pass the sRGB ICC profile [14] to ColorSync to perform correct color correction)

SGI using X

  apply the gamma value from /etc/config/system.glGammaVal (the default value being 1.70; applications running on Irix 6.2 or above may simply pass the sRGB ICC profile to the color management system)

NeXT using NeXTStep

  apply gamma 2.22

"Applying gamma" means that each of the three R, G and B must be converted to $R'=R^{gamma}$, $G'=G^{gamma}$, $B'=B^{gamma}$, before handing to the OS.

This may rapidly be done by building a 256-element lookup table once per browser invocation thus:

```
for i := 0 to 255 do
  raw := i / 255;
  corr := pow (raw, gamma);
  table[i] := trunc (0.5 + corr * 255.0)
end
```

which then avoids any need to do transcendental math per color attribute, far less per pixel.

Appendix E: The Applicability and Extensibility of CSS1

(This appendix is informative, not normative)

The goal of the work on CSS1 has been to create a simple style sheet mechanism for HTML documents. The current specification is a balance between the simplicity needed to realize style sheets on the web, and pressure from authors for richer visual control. CSS1 offers:

- visual markup replacement: HTML extensions, e.g. "CENTER", "FONT" and "SPACER", are easily replaced with CSS1 style sheets.

- nicer markup: instead of using "FONT" elements to achieve the popular small-caps style, one declaration in the style sheet is sufficient. Compare the visual markup:

  ```
  <H1>H<FONT SIZE=-1>EADLINE</FONT></H1>
  ```

  with the style sheet:

  ```
  H1 { font-style: small-caps }
  ```

  ```
  <H1>Headline</H1>
  ```

- various integration levels: CSS1 style rules can be fetched from external style sheets, included in the 'STYLE' element, or put into 'STYLE' attributes. The latter option offers easy transition from HTML extensions.

- new effects: some new visual effects have been added to offer users new toys. The typographical pseudo-elements and the extra values on the background property fall into this category.

- scalability: CSS1 will be useful on equipment ranging from text terminals to high-resolution color workstations. Authors can write one style sheet and be reasonably sure that the intended style will come across in the best possible manner.

CSS1 does not offer:

- per pixel control: CSS1 values simplicity over level of control, and although the combination of background images and styled HTML is powerful, control to the pixel level is not possible.

- author control: the author cannot enforce the use of a certain sheet, only suggest

- a layout language: CSS1 does not offer multiple columns with text-flow, overlapping frames etc.

- a rich query language on the parse tree: CSS1 can only look for ancestor elements in the parse tree, while other style sheet languages (e.g. DSSSL [6]) offers a full query language.

We expect to see extensions of CSS in several directions:

- paper: better support for printing HTML documents

- support for non-visual media: work is in the process to add a list of properties and corresponding values to support speech and braille output

- color names: the currently supported list may be extended

- fonts: more precise font specification systems are expected to complement existing CSS1 font properties.

- values, properties: we expect vendors to propose extensions to the CSS1 set of values and properties. Extending in this direction is trivial for the specification, but interoperability between different UAs is a concern

- layout language: support for two-dimensional layout in the tradition of desktop publishing packages.

- other DTDs: CSS1 has some HTML-specific parts (e.g. the special status of the 'CLASS' and 'ID' attributes) but should easily be extended to apply to other DTDs as well.

We do not expect CSS to evolve into:

- a programming language

Appendix F: Changes from the 17 December 1996 Version

(This appendix is informative, not normative)

This document is a revised version of the CSS1 Recommendation which was first published 17 December 1996 and the list below describes all changes. By selecting the alternate style sheet "errata", all changes will appear highlighted.

We would like to thank Komachi Yushi, Steve Byrne, Liam Quinn, Kazuteru Okahashi, Susan Lesch, and Tantek Çelik for their help in preparing this revised edition.

Spelling and typographic mistakes

- typo1 [section 1.1] The sentence:

  As as result, old UAs will ignore the 'STYLE' element, but its content will be treated as part of the document body, and rendered as such.

  has been changed to:

  As a result, old UAs will ignore the 'STYLE' element, but its content will be treated as part of the document body, and rendered as such.

- typo2 [section 1.6] The sentence:

  The second selector matches matches all 'H1' elements that have an ancestor of class 'reddish'.

  has been changed to:

  The second selector matches all 'H1' elements that have an ancestor of class 'reddish'.

- typo3 [section 2.1] The sentence:

E.g., a style sheet can legally specify that the 'font-size' of an 'active' link should be larger that a 'visited' link, but the UA is not required to dynamically reformat the document when the reader selects the 'visited' link.

has been changed to:

E.g., a style sheet can legally specify that the 'font-size' of an 'active' link should be larger than a 'visited' link, but the UA is not required to dynamically reformat the document when the reader selects the 'visited' link.

- typo4, typo5 [section 2.3–2.4] A trailing quote mark has been added to 'vertical-align'.

- typo6 [section 4] A missing right parenthesis has been added.

- typo7 [section 4.1] A missing comma has been added.

- typo8 [section 4.1.2] The text:

"If more than one of the three is 'auto', and one of them is 'width', than the others..."

has been changed to:

"If more than one of the three is 'auto', and one of them is 'width', then the others..."

- typo9 [section 5.3.6] The word "Examples" has been capitalized.

- typo10 [section 5.4.4] An entity gone astray has been corrected (from "<length&t;" to "<length>").

- typo11 [section 5.5] The text:

The margin properties properties set the margin of an element.

has been changed to:

The margin properties set the margin of an element.

- typo12 [section 5.5.25] Superfluous quote marks have been removed.

Errors

- error1 [section 2.3] A previously invalid declaration (font-style: small-caps) has been replaced by a valid one.

- error2 [section 4] This sentence:

  CSS1 assumes a simple box-oriented formatting model where each element results in one or more rectangular boxes.

  has been replaced with:

  CSS1 assumes a simple box-oriented formatting model where each formatted element results in one or more rectangular boxes.

- error3 [section 4.1] In this sentence:

  The top is the top of the object including any padding, border and margin; it is only defined for inline and floating elements, not for non-floating block-level elements.

  the word "object" has been replaced with "element" to use consistent terminology.

- error4 [section 4.1.3] The alignment of the list items has been corrected.

- error5 [section 4.1.4] There is only one P element in the example, and this sentence:

  Note that the margin of the 'P' elements enclose the floating 'IMG' element.

  has therefore been corrected to:

  Note that the margin of the 'P' element enclose the floating 'IMG' element.

- error6, error7 [section 4.5] The window size can only influence one axis of the canvas, either the width or the height.

- error8 [section 5.4.1] The text inside the parenthesis now refers to a CSS1 property.

- error9 [section 5.4.1] To correspond with the following paragraph, the example has been corrected.

- error10 [section 5.4.8] The section "The height of lines" is now correctly identified as section 4.4, not 4.7.

- error11 [section 5.5] This sentence:

    The 'margin' property sets the border for all four sides while the other margin properties only set their respective side.

  has been corrected to:

    The 'margin' property sets the margin for all four sides while the other margin properties only set their respective side.

- error12, error13, error14, error15, error16, error17, error18, error19, error20, error22 [section 5.5.1–5.5.10] Percentage values refer to width of the closest block-level ancestor, not the parent element (which can be inline) as previously stated.

- error21 [section 5.5.10] Shorthand properties don't have initial values, and the previously specified '0' has therefore been corrected.

- error23 [section 5.5.15] The last rule in the example previously contained an illegal value ('none').

- error24 [section 5.6.6] The value specification on the 'list-style' property had been corrected, but there are no syntactic or semantic changes.

- error25 [section 7.1] The numeric character references used to encode the Greek word "kouros" have been corrected.

- error26 [Appendix A] These element types have been added to the list of selectors attached to the 'display: block' declaration: FORM DL.

- error27 [Appendix B] A dead link to section 7 has been fixed.

- error28 [Appendix D] This text:

    "Applying gamma" means that each of the three R, G and B must be converted to $R'=R^{gamma}$, $G'=G^{gamma}$, $G'=B^{gamma}$, before handing to the OS.

  has been changed to:

    "Applying gamma" means that each of the three R, G and B must be converted to $R'=R^{gamma}$, $G'=G^{gamma}$, $B'=B^{gamma}$, before handing to the OS.

Structure and Organization

- Appendix F, which lists all changes since the 17 December 1996 version has been added.

- A paragraph in the status section has been added to inform readers that this is a revised version.

- The style sheet has changed.

- The reference to a future HTML specification with support for style sheets has been updated to reference HTML 4.0.

- URLs in the References have been updated, and dead links have been removed.

- The underlying HTML markup has been revised.

NOTES

NOTES

NOTES

NOTES

NOTES

NOTES

NOTES

NOTES

NOTES

NOTES

NOTES

NOTES

NOTES